The Hoof And I

A collection of short stories and helpful articles from
the hearts and souls of true horse lovers.

BY LADY MO PASCOE-HOYAL

BY LADY MO PASCOE-HOYAL

WITH GUEST WRITERS: LORD DAVID L. BANKS, PAULA ABBOTT, CHRISTINE RAMSAY, GINGER OTZENBERGER SCHOUEST, VALERIE CURTISS, MELISSA GHRIST RICKER, CHRIS THOMSON, DVM, DALE RACCUGLIA, JODIAH JOHNSON, NORMON C.A. WHYE, MOSIE APPLESEED.

EDITED BY: PAULA ABBOTT

CO EDIT: MO PASCOE-HOYAL

FRONT COVER: GINGER OTZENBERGER SCHOUEST

PHOTO CREDIT: DARYL SCHOUEST

Dedication

To my children, Michael and Jodiah, and to their spouses Linda and Kenny. To my grandchildren, Cameron, McKenzie, Shaylee and Reece. To my great-grand babies, Emery, Blaze, and Aurabella. To all of my family here in Louisiana, and in Tennessee, who have given me nothing but pure love and uplifting encouragement. To my dear family members in Hawai'i, those who remain, and those now sadly gone. To my beloved parents, Charles and Eleanor Pascoe, who are missed... beyond the missing, I wouldn't be who I am if not for you. Special thanks to my husband, "Ivan The Alien," for his support, especially with regard to these #$@%&!* (blankety blank) computers of which I am no whiz; and for the many times he's had to help feed the horses during my often lengthy periods of surgeries and infirmities.

Special Thanks

To the "Little Galoot," my sister, Paula Abbott, Senior Editor, for without her this book wouldn't be possible. Thank you for your unending love, kindness, generosity, and so much patience... and for putting up with me! I sometimes jokingly call you, "You idiot," and this could only happen between two "BFF", sisters, who ultimately love and respect each other; it's more a funny thing we've maintained over the years because we still have the nerve "or freedom" to bring out our silly selves, and we have many times, been silly! The "You idiot" highway runs both ways with us!

We rode our horses, sang and played our music, and together, as backup singers in Nashville, were a team that was hard to beat. Your voice always has, and still adds great life and gusto to anything I do. You now walk another musical road and have become a beautiful vocalist and songwriter in your own right. I am so proud of you! You have been and remain "My Constant," I love you so much, and I thank you from the bottom of YOUR heart, ha, ha!

The Big Galoot!

Paula Abbott, Editor.

Photo Credit: Margaret Slater

Special Thanks

To my dear friend, and adopted "sister," Christine Ramsay, in Eastbourne, East Sussex, England, for her unending friendship and for honoring me with her lovely poem, "A Wonderful Sight To Behold," that she wrote expressly for this book. Christine is a very accomplished Poet. Christine's newly published book: "My Favourite House and other Memories," is a beautiful work of poetic art that is selling well in England.

I send much appreciation to the friends and contributing writers who helped fill in the chapters of this book with their heartfelt stories. Contributing writers: Lord David Lawrence Banks, Valerie Curtiss, Paula Abbott, Norman C. A. Whye, Melissa Ghrist Ricker, Chris Thomson, DVM, Ginger Otzenberger Schouest, Dale Raccuglia, Jodiah Johnson, and Mosie Appleseed. Without you, "The Hoof and I" would remain just a dream.

A very special thank you to Pat Stone, Original Founder and Editor-Publisher of Green Prints- The Weeder's Digest, in accepting my stories for his wonderful publication, and for being a friend to all of his writers and subscribers. Pat is one tough nut to crack as an Editor, and I am honored that he included my stories in his much-loved publication. Special thanks to Green Prints' new Staff and Editor-In-Chief, Don Nicholas, and a new friend there, Deb Kelly. Green Prints has given me the validation I've needed to become a writer! Special special thanks to you brother, Michael L. Hoyal.

In Memory of: Bruce and Linda Nall Maxey, Julie Sermons, Amber Green Eyes, Red Kelly, Norman C.A. Whye, and Tinker B. Bruson.

Table of Contents

Introduction

Perhaps it's odd to title a book "The Hoof And I," however, it's suitable to me because I've been connected to hooves for a very long time, and this can also be taken in the literal sense. The hoof and hooves have been under me as well as all over me! I've looked up to see the belly of a mare, her four legs stomping all over my body that went limp and unconscious beneath her. As you read some of my stories, you'll then understand why I have titled this book as such. The hoof has also carried me to every adventure and misadventure... for decades. I've had a full life and a passion for horses, with whom I still remain in love. Multiple injuries have now rendered me mostly disabled, yet I'm fortunate to still be able to hobble about doing what I can, and to go out to feed and love on my last beloved mare and pony, yes, my very last! Horse people could probably be called some of the nuttiest of the human race because so many of us are just like me; somehow, we keep going. I've always wanted to visit the senior care facility in Hollywood, CA, where old stunt riders go when they can go no more. I'd give anything to be able to compare some stories with those old cowboys, and in spite of our pain and disabilities, I believe I could somehow cheer them up with my kooky horse yarns. I've always wanted "Gunsmoke's" "Festus Haggen" (Ken Curtis) for a best friend. I know so much laughter and "Trickstering" would abound. I would also love to have sung with him. He had a beautiful voice and was once part of the "Sons of the Pioneers" recording group. The old cowboys, how I loved them!

You're born with this love for the horse is all I can say, it's as if the horse is part of you. You can't do without this "craving," it may be some kind of mental defect. It's like an addiction and it never goes away. Ask a musician or an artist, and it's likely they'll tell you the same thing. My friend and former employer, Scotty Moore, once told me, "The music never leaves you."

I hope this effort will bring joy to the readers. There will be sadness, but we also have shown courage, we've given encouragement, sent love, and displayed "unbridled" strength in our endeavors to bring you these stories. Part of our lives and souls now become a part of you. Last but not least...we go out in rain, snow, hail, hurricanes, and tornadoes. We lose our gumboots sometimes to the mud that can suck the boots right off yer feet! We feed, blanket, doctor, and care for these noble creatures... and this has to be nothing but pure love!

I will always remember this quote by Jack Canfield ("Chicken Soup For The Soul.") series creator: "Don't worry about failures; worry about the chances you miss when you don't even try." Mr. Canfield's words of wisdom encouraged me during the many times when the going got rough and during the length of time it took to finish this book. Thank you, Sir!

Lady Mo Pascoe-Hoyal

"I am an Equestropalian, my Cathedral lies under a canopy of trees."

L. Bryant-M. Hoyal

A Wonderful Sight to Behold

There's a picture on my wall

Of a hilltop far away

Where the sun bequeaths its warmth

Upon fields of golden hay.

And there, beyond a rickety fence

'Neath trees leafed in delicate gold

A newborn colt staggers to his feet

Such a wonderful sight to behold.

On shaking legs, he trembles

His downy coat, shiny and wet

His mother nudges him gently

To take his very first step.

He sniffs at the fresh green grass below

And looks around in awe

Remembering all when he is grown

The wonders he once saw.

By: Christine Ramsay-Eastbourne

Chapter 1
Tarka And The Summer Of '74

It's strange looking back now how our own lives are intertwined with animals in times of crisis. Looking out my rear window on this drab November day, my mind drifts back to 1974. It was a hot and humid summer in England. I lived on the outskirts of London near Hertfordshire and Essex. My older sister, Ruth, owned a Connemara pony. She named the pony Tarka, after a popular film that starred an otter of the same name. Tarka was a medium size pony in chestnut brown. She had a dark mane and tail, with white stockings on her legs.

Tarka came over on the ferry from Ireland. After she had been with us for six months, we received an urgent phone call from the landlady of the "Rose and Crown" public house. The pub looked over the field where Tarka was pastured. The landlady said that Tarka had sat down on the grass and hadn't moved for almost a day. I didn't understand the significance of this as I was only ten at the time. It transpired that it is a sign of illness if a horse sits or lies down for any lengthy period of time. The Veterinarian was called, and he rushed over to the field. Tarka was acting very down in the mouth. The Vet diagnosed "Laminitis."

He told us this was very serious and she needed to be walked around for ten minutes every hour and she had to have a special diet. Now, this turned our little family upside-down. My father worked full-time in a hospital in London, and my mother worked as a receptionist. This responsibility of walking Tarka was left to the three of us, Ruth, Norma, and me. Now, Tarka was really Ruth's pony and responsibility, however, Ruth also worked full time as she was older than Norma and me.

Unfortunately, this illness for Tarka happened during mid-term schooling time for us. My parents thought long and hard and decided to take my sister and me out of school for two weeks. Luckily, neither of us was of the exams age yet. So the first fateful day arose, and Norma and I walked the two miles through the woods toward the stables. It was a gloriously hot day and the sun shot light through the dense green canopy above us.

My thoughts were full of next September, which was a huge month for me as I was starting my senior school (High School) and I was filled with trepidation. It was "long trouser" time for me, and the thought of going to a school with over 1,000 other boys was terrifying to me! I would be eleven and the school catered to pupils up to seventeen years of age.

My sister inquired, "What's wrong? You're very quiet." I replied, "Oh, nothing. Just thinking about the big school." Then she said, "Well stop thinking about it, we have Tarka to worry about." I shut out my fears and carried on walking. We eventually got to the stables. I had been given the keys to the main gate, which opened onto the old courtyard. I took the huge key ring and tried the keys until I found which one opened the gate. The rusty iron gate swung open, and we were inside the weathered courtyard with sloping roofs of the centuries-old stables. Tarka was now in a small stall. It was reduced in size, so she couldn't lie down and sleep overnight, which may have killed her. I looked up at Tarka, and her eyes seemed soulful and deep. She looked at us and shifted from side to side against the gnarled wood. Between us, we managed to coax Tarka onto the stones of the courtyard. I could see she was having difficulty in walking. Tarka just stopped and stared at the ground.

I couldn't believe that on the very first day, Tarka decided she didn't want to walk! We tried pulling the leather lead strap attached to her halter. Tarka's hooves remained firmly planted to the ground as she rolled her eyes backward. It was frightening for a young boy to see a pony in such anguish. Physically, Norma and I hadn't a "snowball's chance in hell" of pulling her along. She was a sturdy Irish pony. I was getting down and dismayed. Then, for some reason, I began stroking her long face and speaking in a low, calm tone. Tarka stopped pulling on the lead strap and very gently, I walked in front of her. To my delight and surprise, Tarka walked along behind me.

Then, it suddenly dawned on me that we had to get Tarka back into her stall. We led her to it and very gently pushed her back into the cool brick enclosure. I made a fuss of Tarka and told her what a good girl she was. Norma and I breathed a sigh of relief as we had managed a ten-minute walk around the courtyard. It dawned on me that I had to repeat this for the next eight hours! The sun beat down on us and a light breeze rustled the tall oak trees. I looked at the trees in a slightly different light and for some reason they looked beautiful and graceful as they moved in the warm zephyr. Being with my sister alone, with Tarka, was beginning to have a welcome change in me. For hours Norma and I took turns walking the strong pony round and round the courtyard. Some motorists drove past and waved as the field, and stables could be seen from the roadway.

The owners of the "Rose and Crown" pub came over to us at lunchtime with sandwiches and lemonade. We sat stroking and brushing Tarka as we ate our food. Then, once again, it was back to walking her around the courtyard. I felt so proud that I could lead a pony who was taller than me and clearly could push past me with absolute ease. I hoped in some way that Tarka knew we were trying to save her life. The first day was over, and my father came to pick us up in his Austin Shooting Break. I was tired but felt I had achieved something.

The long hot summer continued and every day Norma and I made our lengthy trek to the stables and walked Tarka around all day. Ten minutes in every hour without fail, we walked the Connemara pony. I found myself looking forward to my time with Tarka. She now gave a snort and whinny when I arrived at her stall. As we walked around I began talking to her about my trepidation of joining high school. To me, what started out as a chore became my first real responsibility at my tender age. We were glad to see Tarka recover from her illness. She was off her medication and back in the fields after two weeks, just as the Vet had predicted.

I still look back on those days with fondness, mostly because of bonding with such a beautiful creature and one who perhaps on one level, knew of the trepidation I felt. As I helped Tarka, she, in turn, helped me accept that I was growing up and was trusted with such a great challenge.

Some may say this is all a figment of my imagination, but to me, it was as real as anything else. Horses are a knowing and wise companion.

Lord David L. Banks

Lord David L. Banks

Chapter 2
Tuning the Young Mind… To Horse Frequency
(Radio Station WHRS)

Keneth Reece Johnson and Ranger

Trying to compare horses to music played on a radio station is a thought most horse owners may not visualize, but to me, this could be a magical combination. I'm a former professional equestrian, musician, published songwriter, and writer, and I've had horses and ponies most of my life. I can watch a Lippizaner go through his paces and think of a lovely waltz. A barrel racer would produce a more frenetic sound, like Rock 'N Roll or Heavy Metal. The Arabian, one of the most graceful and intelligent of breeds in the world, could provoke a magnificent opera, showcasing a powerful voice yet possessing the grace and speed of the cheetah. The "William Tell Overture" reminds me of Thoroughbreds galloping at full speed around the track to the finish line. I won't go down the list in attempting to find more music to match different breeds of horses. I revere both forms of expression, and I love horses with all of my heart.

I first started riding at the age of twelve. It was a full-sized horse I learned to ride on, a big Thoroughbred, and so much better, I thought, than just sitting on the backs of the neighboring teenager's horses when I was eight. I'll always remember the pasture with its long blades of dew-moistened Padequin grass the horses grazed on, verdant and thick, with big juicy stems these horses delighted in, while I sat quietly and pensive upon their backs. I thought about everything around me as I still do now. By the time I reached the age of twelve, I was pretty tall, and as soon as I became a much better rider, I was then "hell bent for leather," afraid of nothing, be it person or horse. I entered many events in English and Western Pleasure, jumping, and was a member of our drill team. I also rode the stable's stallion, "A'li," bareback, all over the place. I seemed to be the only one he allowed to ride him in this manner. "A'li" was a magnificent Arabian stallion, and while he wouldn't let any man enter his stall, he let me in every day for his grooming. I never had any trouble with him because I'd won his trust with kindness, patience, and love instead of the brutality he had endured during breeding from his male handlers, who were loud and abusive to him.

Looking back to my first riding lesson, I realize now that I was totally unprepared. Back then, I was just propped up on a 16 hands-high Thoroughbred and thumped down upon the flat pancake saddle...an English saddle, which was something I'd never seen beyond a horse race. During this first lesson, I sailed off and belly-flopped along the ground. Seeing I wasn't hurt, the instructor told me to get back up. I complied, and from then on, I learned to use my legs and feet as riding and balancing aids. I could have been injured fortunately I was not, but putting a young girl up on a horse in the middle of an outdoor polo field with no barriers and no ground training for both horse and student is not a great way to start! I wasn't "tuned in" nor trained to the ways of the horse. From the onset, I was never cautioned that I would be bitten, kicked, stepped on, bucked off, landed upon, stomped, concussed...and you name it! I didn't learn what I was supposed to do from the ground up and that most accidents in the handling of horses derive from human error. Former information merely consisted of reading a lot of horse novels and watching movies starring the beautiful mounts of my time: Trigger, My Friend Flicka, Black Beauty, and Gallant Bess. (What an astonishing thing it turned out to be when the Hendricks family of the Gallant Bess fame moved to Hawai'i and boarded their famous mounts at our stables, and I became best friends with Lee's daughter, Linda.) All of those perfect Hollywood-trained horses seemed more like fairy tale creatures who would think, do tricks, or save us... didn't compare to the reality of the average horses we had access to, and who, in the presence of danger, would soon as leave us behind in the dust to fend for ourselves.

I've sustained many injuries, and my wonderful world drastically and forever changed if I'd only learned more in the beginning. Careful instruction would more than likely have prevented so many of my accidents and resulting injuries. Permanent disability was too high a price to pay for being untrained in the mannerisms of the horse, and this is why I firmly believe that no one should be put up on a horse and just told to ride before they've reached a decent interval of ground work. In this case, both horse and rider learn together. With my first lesson, cantering came too soon, and this is when I fell off. You don't canter on your first lesson, not in my hard-learned method of training.

Now that I have grandchildren, safety around horses is foremost. I purchased a beautiful Palomino Welsh pony for my nine year old grandson, and we began their training TOGETHER. The topics covered in a three month course which I developed for this beloved boy and his pony completely amazed me in how rapidly he learned, as well as his retention of the lessons. Reece is a fantastic young man, already a good communicator, intelligent "as all get out," and so very handsome! He's mine, and I can sing his praises all day. At first we had to focus on problems, but I was staunch in repetition to make him do as I had asked and for him to do it in the way I in-structured. The first thing I taught him was to go to the "Safe Zone." He'd run to the feed room and, close the wooden gate and stand behind it, as instructed. This, of course, I played up because good and gentle Lolly, whom I've had for years, is a lovely gaited ladies's mount who'd never harm one hair on his head. Welsh pony Ranger, though, may have been another story since I never quite found out how he handled, what was his trail experience, or what his arena manners were like. I noticed his nice little single foot when lunging him, and he looked to be smooth-riding. He could also run like the dickens, stop and turn on a dime. Getting back to horses and children, both can learn to tune into each other, much like how we can tune the radio dial to a certain frequency and enjoy the music.

Mo Pascoe Hoyal and Lolly

Topics covered in the three-month horsemanship class:

1: How to approach a horse, how to properly put on the halter, and where to stand when learning to groom a horse.

2: To observe the signs horses display when annoyed or angered, tired, not feeling well, having sore feet, etc., and "The Safe Zone" for the child to go to when a horse may become fractious. This was hilarious for us and fun because none of our horses here are fractious, but still..."a horse is a horse, of course, of course." Temperament should never be taken for granted. We'd practice "fractious horse" and I'd say with alarm, "Ranger is starting to behave badly, run to the safe zone!" Reece would run to the safe confines of the feed room, shut the gate and look out at me and grin. However, he did take this very seriously.

3: General anatomy, to name and point to, paper test afterward

4: The basics: How to pick up a hoof and to pick it out. Lead the horse, walk in circles, and backing up. We set up a minor course where poles were placed on the ground and comfort spaced for hooves and feet, fitting for both pony and student to learn to step over together.

5: Feeding and nutrition, mucking stall and paddock, barn and feed room clean-up, and how much to feed and when. Actual "hands-on" experience with the Farrier and Veterinarian who worked on our horses, both of which were very enlightening to my grandson.

6: Riding bareback in circles in a confined paddock space. This came last.

I had a very apt pupil. Becoming enlightened with "hands-on" techniques and visual training made an impression on this young boy and a sometimes gnarly and not-so-little Welsh pony. This training time spent also helped a gentle and loving aging mare who followed us around unhaltered at every step. She got praised just as much and is one who had to be pretend doctored, along with Ranger if he had a scratch or injury! It was especially helpful for a disabled, oft times depressed former equestrian and grandmother as well.

Teaching young children is a very rewarding experience both for child and instructor. Horses, and "tuning in" to them is vital for anyone of any age, and is essential to getting along with your horse while also asserting yourself through kindness. A fine example of this training can be seen in the way Clinton Anderson works with all horses. I admire Clinton very much. The term "Horse Whisperer" is, and has been, too loosely given to people who simply watch and who are patient, kind, and "in tune" to the ways of the horse. All "Horse Whisperers" I've seen use a similar technique, which is kindness instead of violence, as was used in the old days of cowboy training when the spirit of the horse was broken many a time. Unfortunately, that still exists. If one is not old enough to remember this adage, it's a good one, "You can attract more flies with honey than you can with vinegar." You can count on this as a good way to handle your own affairs throughout life, and it's a kind way of life that will generally work for you, your human, and your animal friends.

Lady Mo Pascoe-Hoyal

Photo Credit:

Mo Pascoe – Hoyal

Wayne E. Hoyal.

Chapter 3
Radar

I first met Radar, probably three or four days after Hurricane Rita hit the coast of Calcasieu Parish in south Louisiana, September of 2005. Radar was a rescue horse, and when I first saw him, I quickly noticed that half of the skin on his head was missing. He was cut from his top-notch all the way across, and it had pulled an ear back all the way down. His eyelids were re- moved on one side. Halfway down his forehead, the skin was still there; it was just peeled back. I thought, let's try to fix this and see what we can do. I've always said that a horse's head will heal very well; you just have to try and sew it up.

Radar, I guessed, was a Thoroughbred crossbreed, stood 16 hands...a pretty big horse, and as you can imagine, he was pretty flighty after being caught in a hurricane and then left with his wound untreated for several days. So, after we cleaned it, I started trying to stitch it up and realized it was just really, really tight! I was able to apply sutures to replace the skin around the eye, and as we started pulling it and then dividing dead tissue and what not, it got really tight! The ear was cut off right at the base by the ear canal, and muscle attachment was severed. We really didn't have hope this would heal but I kept suturing, and slowly, slowly, slowly, pulling piece by piece, until I finally got it reapposed and him looking like a normal horse again.

To this day I don't know what this horse's name was but I called him Radar after we were done because his ear stood straight up just like a horse standing at attention. Looking ahead, however, he couldn't move it and I had hoped that in time, the ear would gain motion so it would move. Unfortunately, over a period of time, as it scarred in, his ear never did regain any motion and was very stiff. But I guess, considering the circumstances, it was better to have an ear that stood stiff, with an eyelid that couldn't blink, than having no eyelid at all. Although things looked pretty dire, and with the probability that many people would just have put him down, Radar lived a "happily ever after" life with his erect ear and eyelid that couldn't blink very well.

Chris Thomson, DVM

Chapter 4
Under The Influence...Of Horses!

As a child and young adult, I was timid, but being on a horse made me feel very large and very much in charge! I was always around these wonderful animals since my sister worked at a local stable and had horses in her care. She created an environment for me to get to know the horses we so loved, none of them ours, but ones we rode for others. Mo turned me loose one day on an old paint named Comanche, and we plodded around the grounds together near Kapi'olani Park, which was right across the road from Ala Moana beach. I checked in with her every once in a while just so she knew I was safe. It was truly a good day...and not so bad a place to grow up as well! Later, I was introduced to the remarkable Polo pony and would "hot walk" them during the matches between chukkers. Man, that was great, walking these horses to cool them down after they ran at break neck speeds for the athletes from Argentina, Australia, our local horsemen of Hawai'i and Oh, a visiting Prince Phillip from the United Kingdom, you know, the Queen's hubby!

After graduating high school, I worked a couple of jobs, but nothing very fulfilling. Mo had moved away to the deep south, where she had begun raising her family. When she came back to the islands for a visit, she suggested I go back with her to her home in Louisiana. After a struggle for permission from my parents, I was finally allowed to leave. I was nineteen at the time and needed to broaden my horizons. It was then I learned the western style of riding. Sis arranged to get a small, green-broke mare for me, about the age of six, and a grey roan in color. I named this horse Shalimar after the perfume, and I was in love! We had a symbiotic relationship. Shalimar taught me to be a better rider while I put her through her paces. I had a new found freedom and felt very connected to this wonderful rhythm between my horse and me. We'd go on trails all over the area, and I always felt safe. Often, we took those walks along the highway to the burger joint for a refreshing drink for me and a treat of an ice cream cone for Shalimar from the owner of the establishment. Life was good!

But then, one day, I took my steed on a different route. To my dismay, I found the shoulder of the little back road to be very narrow and uncomfortably close to on-coming vehicles. At one spot, Shalimar became a bit spooked and hopped sideways. To my misfortune, sideways was a mailbox. The hem of my pants got hooked onto the latch of the mailbox door, and Shalimar wouldn't stop so I could get free. Together, we pulled that thing over, post and all. Knowing I should do the right thing, I got her calmed down, and we went looking for the owner, who lived down a long driveway in a little subdivision. Shalimar and I found the woman and her two children at home. I dismounted, and we stepped under the carport to make our amends. She was understanding and not at all angry, especially when I offered my brother-in-law's services of putting her mailbox to the right. That being arranged, the horse, who then acted on nature's call, took the liberty of depositing a healthy heap of dung onto the woman's freshly swept carport floor. Well, that was the straw that broke this poor camel's back, which colored my face a vivid shade of humble. All this woman did was silently hand me a shovel and pail. I did my duty, scooped up the horse doody, and quietly rode back home. I learned humility that day. Sometimes you train a horse, some- times a horse trains you! As time passed, I realized that I needed a car more than I needed my horse. I couldn't ride my horse to my job at the dime store up the highway, so I sold my little mare and got enough from the transaction to put a down payment on another ride, this time a 1963 Ford Galaxy with a 390 T-Bird engine. It was a fantastic new experience to be able to go anywhere, on pavement that is, and a lot farther as well.

Fast forward five years, and there I was with a young son, living less than a mile from my sister, and what did she do? She asked if I wanted to keep her bay mare at my place since she had another horse and pony on her property to take care of. The horse I accepted had a Hawai'ian name, of course, and this mare was called Maile' after the fragrant green leaves strung into leis and worn originally by the royals of Hawai'i-the Ali'i. My son, Brandon, was only two at the time, but he'd wait patiently while I saddled Maile' and then mounted. Brandon would stand next to her and reach up to me as I leaned down and picked him up to seat him in front of me and then I'd hand him the reins. We went on our regular ride around the three-mile circle. Marauding neighborhood dogs were always on their rant and so they followed and barked the whole time we were in their territory. But the gentle bay mare just kept her head and went on without being bothered by these coon hounds. Remember, I was in Louisiana, a very rural area with no leash laws, and hunting raccoons was very much the "in sport" for many. Who recalls Jerry Clower? He did a whole comedy routine on coon hunting.

Getting back to the trail, Brandon and I rode a lot together. It was such a great thing to be on a horse with my little boy, and although he held the reins for a good part of our ride, Maile' knew the route, and we were happy just walking along. Brandon felt in control for a little while, a rarity for a two-year-old, right? I jest, we all know who's in control when there's a toddler around. Those were some of the most peaceful days of my life until Maile' got out of her paddock and meandered on over to a neighbor's house. I got a phone call...."Your horse is down here eating my flowers," she said in dismay. I had to catch Maile' and lead her back home. Well, some of the time was peaceful! I miss those days.

After a failed marriage, I moved Brandon, my dog, my bird, and a few house plants and clothing, all in a 1970 Mustang, and drove up to Nashville. The household goods and furniture were sent by moving van. The only horses I've ridden since were stubborn, old rental horses that were barn sour and ruined by everyone else who sometimes didn't know one end from the other.

However, both ends are dangerous! After marrying a second time and to a good man who raised Brandon as his own son, I gave birth to another son, Ian. I'm sorry I didn't have a horse at the time, but that's how life is. There were different things to keep me busy-a job being one, although always third on my list of importance. Ian did get to ride his cousin's horse when he visited Texas and came back telling us all about it. It was then Ian had a happy insight into many of my former experiences with horses.

The influence of the horses in our lives was huge and anyone who has the good fortune of being around them will understand. I love them still, and watch events that come on TV involving horses. Football, I'm sure has its merits, baseball and soccer too, but these don't interest me at all. Now I go into the "Memories Vault" and relive the days when the simple pleasure of riding a horse could throw me back to that time I was in Mrs. Rich's Equitation class, and when we were told to trot our horses. I lost my balance during one lesson and went over the side onto a thickness of sawdust. My mount came to an abrupt stop and as I lay there, Hula Girl put her nose to my face. I've always thought she was checking to see if I was alright.

I have held these magnificent animals in high esteem my entire life, admiring their beauty and grace, their strength and courage. Steeds who once bore the ancients into battle, or carried historians and explorers to new lands, and others who sped princes into the Polo grounds. I've not had the pleasure of being on a horse in ages, but I

21

now drive a pickup with 350 horses under the hood. There's no getting away from the power of the horse; it's built into the vehicles we drive.

I must stop here and tell you that my love for family has always come first, yet the love for a horse and the companionship it brings cannot compare with anything else that I know.

Paula Abbott

Chapter 5
Hoof Prints On The Heart

My parents were wonderful and gave me everything they could. I was healthy and smart. Having two brothers and two sisters, I was definitely not lonely. I had no disabilities, but I was shy. Doesn't sound so bad, right? Of all the things to complain about, it seems like a minor thing, yet it was so debilitating at times. I had no confidence and was lost in a world of people I desperately wanted to be with, but I always felt like an outsider. Was I invisible? It seemed like no one saw me. No one disliked me; no one really liked me either. It was as though I just didn't exist, and it was rough on a young girl trying to navigate her way through life.

Horses changed my life. I'm not sure how I "found" horses, though I'm certain I was meant to. No one in my family had ever touched one. I think it happened to me at a little county fair when I rode a pony named Red around and around in circles. I didn't want to go to the fair that day...mostly because I was uncomfortable in social situations, but as I said, it was meant to be. I was eight years old, and after that day, horses were my passion, although I didn't have one yet. In my mind, I was already an equestrian. I clipped pictures from magazines and covered my bedroom walls with them. I checked out as many books from our local library as my mom would allow. Riding alone on the school bus or being the lone diner during lunch no longer bothered me. My dreams now overwhelmed most of my waking hours, and I couldn't care less about my social status.

The next summer, my parents enrolled me in a horse camp. I guess they still thought it was a phase at this point. The week-long adventure fueled my obsession, and even the social aspect at camp didn't bother me so much. After the week was over, I started cleaning stalls at the farm that held the camp. I would wake my dad at the crack of dawn and beg him to drop me off at the farm. There, I'd stay all day long until my mom picked me up on her way home from work. I worked for free, and it was hard work. I mucked stalls, groomed, bridled and saddled horses, polished tack...you name it, I did it. Occasionally, I would get to ride a horse. After summer ended, I rode the bus from school to my "job." My parents were outraged that I was working for nothing, but it didn't matter to me. Just breathing in the scent of the horse was payment enough. I was a fanatic!

I made it all the way to fifth grade before my parents relented and bought me a horse. They must have realized I wasn't going to change my mind anytime soon. A young mare was the first horse we looked at. She was dark brown with a white stripe down her nose. A tiny girl she was, standing at just 14.2 hands and petite like me. No registration papers accompanied her; we couldn't afford that, but I didn't care. I had my own horse! We named her Cyanna. She didn't have any training, and neither did I. It should have been a recipe for disaster, but it wasn't. We learned together. I never thought of Cyanna as my possession; she was more of a partner to me. Perhaps that's why we were so wildly successful.

I joined 4H and started attending any event I could possibly make it to. Nearly every day, Cyanna and I would train and ride. The poor horse worked hard, but she always seemed to enjoy it and never refused in any way. Before too long, we were competing at 4H events and horse shows. This miraculous horse competed in everything from barrel racing- to jumping at some point in her life. Cyanna was a fraction of the size of most horses out there, but her heart was double their size. We consistently beat the larger horses that bore their registration. We didn't have fancy tack, and we never needed any of that stuff.

I started to come out of my shell shortly after getting Cyanna. All of a sudden, I was happy. Speaking up in class and even making a few friends the next year came easier. I'd always brought home good grades, but something changed, and I began to realize my potential. Every time I heard our names called over the loud speaker announcing a ribbon, a small part of the in- visible girl grew brighter. It was as if my first success with Cyanna brought to light that I was worth more than I ever thought possible.

Cyanna got a friend a couple of years later. A two-year-old horse came running (literally) into our lives one afternoon. He had gotten loose from his property a few blocks away. Every bone was visible, and his coat was dull and unhealthy looking. His hooves were cracked, and his tail had been chopped or torn off. He was a pathetic sight, but his eyes were full of life and desire. Despite his obvious abuse, he was so excited to be out running free. After some negotiation with his owners (and my parents,) I now had a second partner, who we named Scorpio after one of my favorite race horses. Scorpio's road to recovery was long, but soon after, Scorpio and I were also in the ribbons. He blossomed into a beautiful horse.

Scorpio and Cyanna were inseparable, and I was the happiest girl around! My life was full, and I couldn't have asked for more. The three of us grew up together. I learned much more from those two horses than they ever learned from me.

I was awarded a scholarship to Texas A&M University, where I studied and eventually earned my Master's Degree in Nuclear Engineering. Cyanna and Scorpio made the trip with me, and spent my college years at a nearby stable. Our competitive riding transitioned into trail riding on the weekend. After graduating six years later, the three of us moved south to start our new lives. The horses now mostly enjoyed their retirement. At this point, they more than deserved it. As busy as I was with my new job, there was never a day I let go of my passion for horses.

Life moved on, and the three of us moved several times over the next six years. Changing jobs, getting married, moving to different houses...we went through a lot together. Even though the horses were in full retirement at this point, they were just as big a part of my life as they always had been. I lost Scorpio first in 2011. It was sudden and unexpected. I was devastated, I still am. Cyanna stood over his grave for days. Never let anyone tell you that animals cannot mourn. Then, I lost Cyanna in 2013. Those horses had been my family for over twenty years. They are now galloping around the fields of Heaven together, waiting patiently for me to join them someday. To them, I owe my success, my happiness, and my ability to overcome anything that gets in my way. Without those two horses, I would still be hidden inside a terrified little child. I wouldn't have gotten to experience life and success. They taught me confidence, responsibility, dedication, and love.

I don't know that I will ever have the same connection to another horse, I hope I will. Now, over a year later, three beautiful young horses grace my barn. I love them. I don't know if they'll teach me as much as Cyanna and Scorpio did, but maybe they will teach my child someday. If they do, that child will be as fortunate and blessed as I am. And if that child is really lucky, he or she will someday have permanent hoof prints on the heart... just like mama does.

Melissa Ghrist Ricker

Chapter 6
A Bit Of A Stirrup Saves An Unfortunate Grasper

A bit of fiction from Merry Olde England

"Did I tell you about the horse with the golden shoes?" The elderly recluse eyed me up with a look that was both half smiling and piercing. When I glared at him inquisitively, he glowered, then with a wry smile that had seen many years of every change of the weather, a succession of every judicial government of the last eighty years, and the inside of most prisons in the eastern counties, and had steadfastly remained in dominant of them, he said, "He had trodden on the streets that have been paved with gold!"

His clear blue eyes in the wizened, stubbly, tanned face gleamed with mischief as he lit his old meerschaum pipe, which looked as if he had been born with it and never gone out for most of his ninety years. He puffed out a cloud of aromatic smoke and, with another wry smile, uttered, "Yes! You can take old Samson for a ride; he needs some exercise, and he knows you well, but take care of him and bring the both of you back in time for tea." He stomped off through his old homemade gate and stroked Jesse, his large tabby cat, who immediately rose up, arched his back with pleasure, and resumed his position of guard on the garden seat near the front door.

"Thank you Arthur, I will." I reined Samson out of the small field and set off at a gentle trot across the little lane and on to the dunes towards the ruins of Donstint Church, which as we neared it seemed to be as knarled and weather-worn as the elderly reclusive Arthur, who had disappeared into his cottage at the edge of the dunes.

The dunes gave way to the pine forest, and we relaxed a bit. Samson knew the forest and the trodden walkways well, as I had ridden him several times through this unspoiled nature reserve with its chorus of rooks, which were noisily constructing nests in the tops of the trees. Their raucous squabbling for ownership of their chosen tree gave a constant background of noisy competition. When we stopped at the gate, I dismounted, eased Samson through, and after I had closed it as I had found it...as the Country Code demanded, I remounted Samson, and we trotted easily over the dunes towards Donstint Village.

Donstint Village was small. A dozen houses, a shop, a pub, and a small chapel were segregated from the new housing estate that was situated about a mile from the old ruin of the church. During a tempestuous storm, the sea had completely wiped out everything, drowning terrified villagers and leaving a medley of devastated ruins of all homesteads, gardens, fields, and lanes. The insurance company had replaced several of the homes and then liaised with the parish council to build a council estate at least two miles inland from the original village. There were some protests, but the authorities were adamant, and the result was that most of the inhabitants were placed on the council estate. Only a handful of the original surviving residents lived in the actual village, as their homes had suffered little damage from the tempest.

We branched off the road and went down a narrow track leading to the beach and then to the tank traps (solid concrete cubes about four feet square, irregularly placed to impede the advancement of invading enemy tanks and artillery in the event of a Nazi invasion in the last war.) The track meandered through to a small allotment estate and wound through a stream and down to the beach, a good ride for

Samson, with the chance of a paddle in the incoming surf as the tide encroached the beach road.

The raucous scream of a frightened Herring gull nesting amongst the concrete cubes caused Samson to rear up in alarm. Not being as alert as I should have been, I flipped out of the saddle and landed on the corner of one of the tank traps. A bolt of searing pain shot through my leg, and I saw a flashing light before landing awkwardly between the uneven row of concrete cubes. I saw Samson galloping over the nearby dune and then all went into blackness.

What seemed to be an eternity, but in reality was only a few minutes, the blackness cleared and I began to take stock of my position and surroundings. I had banged my head, but the ache was already clearing. However, my right leg was hot, and any attempt to move it shot more agony through it. I called Samson, but there was no friendly reply. It was the first time I had ridden him through the traps and in these parts of the dunes. There was no response to my calls, and I knew I was a long way from any human habitation. The incoming tide was not lending a chance of meeting any wandering beach-comber and was steadily approaching the high tide line left from the previous evening.

The disturbed gull had returned to her nest but was also giving a cold eye to my predicament. My leg was bleeding and going numb. I was not in any situation to move quickly, and I couldn't see any driftwood sticks or nearby stony rocks to be used as a crutch or a weapon against the gull's increasing interest in my wounded leg. She had been sitting on her nest for some time and the finding of seafood, discarded picnic debris, or lunch wrappings and uneaten remains were not readily available. A wounded animal was fair game for a healthy, hungry nesting gull-and the only nearby wounded animal was me! I called Samson again, but no friendly whinny replied. Night was fast approaching, and night meant forage time for opportune feeders like sea gulls. Cold was also slowly becoming apparent, and the prospect didn't look all that rosy for a disabled, bleeding animal, let alone a human one!

As the darkness of a clouded sky descended, I felt panic rising like a thunder cloud after a blistering hot summer day. I called Samson again and again, quickly changing to asking for anybody in ear shot. The hen Gull's mate had appeared, and the pair was eying my situation with far too much interest for my liking. I could not feel my leg, and the chill was invading my body. I was also hoarse from shouting, and the loneliness was extremely acute. I tried to keep awake by singing to myself, but despondency was prevalent. I imagined a lump of discarded remains with fat, marauding, sated gulls inquisitively pecking at any leftover morsel... of me!

Suddenly I became aware of warm breathing at my ear. I opened my eyes and saw a large shadow snuffling at my face. I moved my arm and felt a warm animal coat and a nose investigating my leg, and then Samson was inquisitively nuzzling my face. I tried to speak, but only a groan emerged. Things at this point didn't look too enterprising. Samson was very inquiring, and I felt too cold to acknowledge any feelings in return. I tried to shout but only a whisper came forth.

Slowly, the big horse knelt down on his front knees and followed with his back legs. He carefully rolled to me till I could feel his rugged body touching mine. I felt the stirrup close to my hand, and gripping it tightly, I held on. Samson then very carefully rolled over until I was on his back. I grasped both the stirrup and the girth. Very slowly, the horse rose steadily to his knees, and gently, I was lifted off the ground and up over his mid-back. I suddenly remembered an old American cowboy film where the hero took the dead villain back over to the sheriff and thought of the gun belt with one bullet missing from it, but I was dreaming. Samson slowly walked forwards and kept that pace with me dangling across his back.

Suddenly, I perceived voices. Some people were gently lifting me down, and blue flashing lights lit up the area. Then, all was dark again.

I woke in a comfortable bed; a lot of activity was about. I saw my leg set straight and heavily bandaged and a nurse hovering inquiringly. A man in a white lab coat with a stethoscope slung round his neck was looking at me.

"Ah! You are awake at last! You were in the right state when you were brought in here. How come you have sand and vegetation all over you? You were nowhere near the beach. We picked you up out of old Mr. Smitcher's garden-he keeps his garden immaculate. It's not got any of that sea-thistle stuff anywhere near it! And how did you arrive there with a broken leg as badly as that? There was no one else around when he called us!"

Norman C. A. Whye

Chapter 7
Darling Dynamite

While pondering my youth, it always seemed that growing up would take forever. I think back to the long summer days and how they would pass so slowly, like molasses dripping. We dwindled away our early days, clueless to how quickly the years would sprint by later in our adult-hood, like a thief in the night. Ultimately...time is a thief, I accuse!

A particular period in my life which I visit in my mind, the vault that holds many of the greatest memories, is when I return to the days of my youth with my Darling Dynamite.

Dynamite, my "midget horse" as I affectionately thought of him, was, in reality, a fully grown Shetland pony. He was my best friend in those days. Imagination would freely run wild in my eight-year-old brain. We'd go to the days of the Old West and how life might have been when the Cowboys and Indians ruled the prairies. Dynamite somehow managed to keep me balanced and out of trouble.

This girl was somewhat a tomboy, yet feminine as well. I appreciated my dolls, tea sets, and let's not forget the paper dolls with the endless wardrobe options. But on the other hoof...I was gone like the wind on that pony from morning and sometimes 'til dusk when Mom would make us come in. Yes, our curfew was the appearance of lightning bugs. The world was a relatively safer place back then, unlike today, so Mom didn't worry too much.

Let me just say that Dynamite and I had some adventures. Think of Huck Finn without the river. I ate, drank, and slept at times on his back, so comfortably. I was never a fan of saddles and bridles, although mom, the lifelong horse whisperer, had a plethora of them hanging in her barn for other beloved horses. I rode Dynamite bareback, being the rebel I am, and had a special way of mounting, which entailed running up from behind him and basically leapfrogging onto his back. He was always trusted to stand there, just as still as could be, to assure my safe landing. I was ever so careful to avoid his flanks because most horse people know what happens then (a horse usually kicked in its flanks will buck.) I would grab a big lock of that black, coarse mane, gave a little kick and a nudge, and we'd be off, happily traipsing across the countryside, tapping into my imagination of what world we would sample on that particular day. We were always careful to stay within the perimeters of the cattle gaps down the road, as it was a free range in our small town of Pollock, Louisiana. Our neighbor's cows, much to my mother's dismay, roamed freely wherever their hearts so desired, and sometimes they went straight for the "buffet" of mom's garden in which she worked so hard. My mother, the nature lover, always had that green thumb thumping and things growing like mad. Presently, her beloved animals bring a sense of sanity to her as this world gets crazier by the minute.

Gone are the days of my Darling Dynamite. Marriages fail, parentsdivorce, and children grow up and move on with life. The one thing I will always cherish and keep alive inside me, never to forget, is the spirit of that special animal in my life, way back then, tucked away in a dimension of time when life was sweet and I hadn't a care in the world. This was my special time, lazing away those long summer days with my friend, my special boy, my Darling Dynamite.

Jodiah Johnson

Chapter 8
The Stirrup, A Most Necessary Invention

Part One

Riding bareback always came easy for me. I loved and cherished the freedom and contact with the animal underneath, which was exhilarating for the dare devil rider that I was! Before becoming a horse owner, myself, I rode for Polo clubs and for owners of many other horses of varied breeds. One horse in particular that I well remember was a Polo Pony named Leilani (Heavenly Flower,) and this she was. We lived in Hawai'i, and life was grand! This mare would have been an award-winning mount in English and Western Equitation, Hunter Hack, jumping, and just a darned good all-around horse. I rode her bareback with only a hay string loosely tied around her bottom jaw. Of all the ponies I rode and cared for, Leilani and I bonded like no other. I wish I could have purchased her, but at age sixteen, earning $300.00 was like trying to get $3,000.00. I still miss that gorgeous creature, I also miss the strength and agility I had in my youth.

As much as I love to ride bareback, these days, I'm confined to riding in this manner in my small paddock. A total insult! And, with much contempt for old age approaching way faster than I had wanted. I remain safe in my Australian saddle with its frontal build-up that keeps me in it. The importance of the stirrup for added comfort and strength given to the rider has made an incredible difference in the history of riding, and without it, many of us would easily be tossed into the brush.

Curiously enough, while entertaining thoughts of writing an article about the importance of stirrups, I happened upon a television documentary shown on the History Channel (name of show not remembered. Aha, I can now claim "senior moments.") This show was relevant to the importance of the stirrup in Medieval times when jousting was all the rage. Modern testing proved what a tremendous difference the addition of the stirrup made.

Back then, a board placed on a pole was constructed to measure the strength of the thrust with and without the support of the stirrup. Prior to using a stirrup, the amount of force leveled at point of impact was approximately 31.5%. With the use of stirrups, the impact the pole had on the board soared to 90%. What a remarkable contrast in how stirrups had upped the score to such a degree. From that point forward, jousting was performed only with the addition of stirrups.

It's said the stirrup, when invented, was originally used in and around the Jin Dynasty, China, circa 322 BC, for the sole purpose of mounting. They list from 265 through 420 BC for the sole purpose of mounting; however, terra cotta warriors and horses of the Qin Dynasty 206-221 BC that were unearthed in the Lin Tong District in Northwest China's Shaanxi Province showed the invention of some kind of stirrup, and in what time period it came to be. However, controversy remains as to who invented them.

"Few inventions have been so simple as the stirrup, but few had such a catalytic influence on history. The requirements of the new mode of warfare, which it made possible, found expression in a new form of western European society dominated by an Aristocracy of warriors endowed with land so that they may fight in a new and specialized way."

Imagine the rising feudal class of the Middle Ages and how they came to the ultimate form by the use of two stirrups. Something so simple, yet something so necessary.

Lady Mo Pascoe-Hoyal

*Reference quote from Lynn White's "Medieval Technology and Social Change," 1966

Chapter 9

The Stirrup: A Most Necessary Invention

Part Two

It's noted, but not proven, that the horse wasn't domesticated until 4000 BC. Before this, the smaller pre-horse sizes were eaten. The Eohippus was the size of a fox, and there were two more evolutions; the Mesohippus and the Protohhippus, until the horse evolved large enough to be ridden and used for work and war. There is proof of types of blankets and crude saddles with circingles (girths) approximately between 500-800 BC. In India, at about the same period, there was merely a piece of rope tied in a circle, small enough to fit only the big toe of a barefoot rider, hanging from the left side of the horse. So it seems odd to me that other research indicates the horse wasn't domesticated until 4000 BC. Therefore, controversy still exists in my mind as to who first invented the stirrup and when the horse was initially domesticated and ridden?

During the first and second centuries, carvings of horseman were depicted riding on elaborate saddles with their feet tucked into the girth. That sounds incredibly uncomfortable and unsafe. Next came the invention of a solitary stirrup fixed onto the left side of an early form of saddle, which was used as a mounting aid by nomads known as the Sarmatians.

While doing research to pinpoint the exact origin of the stirrup and who first came out with it, the search became to intensive and contained so many differing opinions; it's no wonder there's ongoing controversy as to just exactly when the stirrup came to be. It's possible, though, that riders in many parts of the world came to the same conclusion or invention, much like what happens today. People in different parts of the world come up with the same inventions, ideas, chord progressions, and similar lyrics for songs, books or movie titles, and it basically boils down to whoever gets the first patent or copyright is the one who will get the credit and monetary payoff.

Various uses of stirrups according to the different styles of riding:

Track racing: Shortened stirrups are used by jockeys and have light-weight stirrup irons. The shortened stirrups enable the jockey to stay better balanced over the middle of the back of a galloping mount in order to help the horse reach the fastest speed possible.

Dressage: "The execution by a horse to do complex maneuvers in response to barely perceptible movements of a rider's hands, legs, and weight." The stirrups are set longer where the leg shows no uplift. (Quote: Webster's New Collegiate Dictionary, G & C Merriam Company, Springfield, MA).

Stirrups used in timed events such as barrel racing, roping, pole bending are pulled up to an intermediary length, giving the rider a slightly bent knee, making it easier to stand up if necessary, or to dismount faster.

Jumping: For the jumper, stirrups play a large role in helping the rider to have greater balance while going over 6' or plus hurdles. These stirrups have ridges at the knees as an aid for keeping the legs in a better position. English, Dressage, and jumping saddles are essentially the same, with the exception of slight modifications.

If stirrups didn't exist, ancient riding would have been dangerous and uncomfortable. This invention changed the outcome of warfare...the victors had stirrups! There's a downside to stirrups that are permanently fixed to a saddle, as with some of the older Western saddles. It's possible for the rider's leg or foot to get caught in them and being unable to get out of a perilous situation. Thanks to another great invention, there's now a break-away stirrup that comes off with the leg when the rider begins to fall. Serious injury or even death can be averted when using these stirrups.

The stirrup gives greater stability to a rider and is considered to be one of the most significant inventions in the development of riding gear. The stirrup was also considered as important as gunpowder, the wheel, and the printing press! Imagine that...something so simple, yet so necessary. What I can't envision, though, is trying to ride with only a big toe in a small loop while galloping full speed ahead!

Lady Mo Pascoe-Hoyal

Chapter 10
The Donkeys, Ponies, And Horses In My Life

At the age of seventy-threethere are no large, four-footed beings in my life. As an artist, I have painted one or two, but actual riding and horse husbandry are subjects of which I know little, so when my Louisiana "sister" asked me to write about the horses in my life, I was thinking how to do that and make it more than one-page long.

My first experience with donkeys, ponies, and horses came when I was five years old and had just moved to Hunstanton, a seaside town in the county of Norfolk, England. This is the same county whichproduced Princess Di-we were both Norfolk "broads." We lived at first in a beach bungalow while my parents looked for a house large enough to contain a Private school. Now that would have been hunky dory in the balmy days of a short English summer, but this was February, and ice shrouded the windows of this non-insulated summer domain. All of that aside, I awoke the first morning to the braying of donkeys. I diligently scraped off enough ice from the window to be able to see out. It was with much delight (remember, I was only five) that I realized the beach donkeys and ponies were quartered in a field right behind the bungalow. During that winter, I had to settle for petting them from over the fence, where they took my meager offerings of carrots or apples, and I would have to wait for summer when each day the owner would take his four-footed stock to the beach to "hire them out" for sixpence a ride, which is the equivalent of ten cents back then. That was a long time ago!

It was with great anticipation that one could scrounge up the said pennies for the realization of getting to ride one of these gentle beasts. The donkeys were the cheapest rides, slow of gait and plodded along, but it was much more thrilling to ride a genuine pony! Money was tight in those days, and one didn't often have the where with all to be able to ride a real horse up and down the beach. The six pence would only take you between one set of groynes-sand erosion barriers which were about 100 yards apart and not far at all for a ride, it seemed.

With a few years under my belt, my mother had enrolled me in riding lessons in Heacham, several miles down the road. Yes, it was the English style, with a complete riding habit that entailed a black velvet hard hat, tan jodphurs, yellow knit turtle neck jumper (sweater) and of course, the necessary riding crop. I guess our money never stretched to the leather boots or the velvet jacket. I used to bicycle down the steep hill that stretches from Hunstanton to Heacham to arrive at the stables, whereby one had to learn the names of all the tack, learn to groom the horse, saddle and bridle him, and then finally get to mount and ride in a large covered ring. We learned the necessary gaits of walk, trot and canter. Once in a while, we got to trail ride, but those times were very few and far between. I was always wary, a reader, not a doer, never the brave daredevil soul, and much more in love with ballet and tap than horsemanship. When it got to the point where we had to learn to jump, I chickened out. As the jumps got higher and higher, I just knew that the horse was going to plant his hooves firmly into the dirt right before the jump, and I, being light-weight, would just keep on going. Luckily, at about that time, the money for lessons had run out. The most thrilling and memorable moment I had ever experienced was when I was about eleven. The circus came to town, and with it all the excitement and intrigue that a circus could drum up in an impressionable and romantic young girl. During the show, the time came for the equestrian act. Several beautiful ladies entered and were garbed out in sparkling sequins and tights. Trick riders who could stand on the horse's back, or Romans ride two horses (one foot on each while turning somersaults and jumping) as the horses went through their maneuvers around the ring. Then came the most exciting part. They called for kids to come up and give it a try...to stand up and ride on one of the horses! I threw my hand up and of course, yelled, "me, me, me!" and was lucky enough to get chosen. The excitement bubbled as they buckled me into a safety harness with a tether that ran through a ring at the roof of the Big Top, then back to a circus hand who held onto the rope. They hoisted me up onto the horse and slowly, we trotted around the ring. Next, it was time to swing my legs up behind me and, get onto my knees, and finally take that big step up, arms akimbo, letting the movements of the horse define that little jump. Then, all too soon, the sliding fall, the pull of the stage hand, and I was flying around the ring on the end of the tether! I was gently let to the floor and boy, was I ready to join the circus!

My world of horse riding took a back seat for many years and didn't start up again until I was married, emigrated to the U.S.A., and had produced four children. We decided in 1974, when the World Expo was held in Spokane, WA, that it would be fun to take the kids on a trail ride held in the area. That was quite a fiasco as my most daring child had the luck to be given a horse that had nothing else on his mind than to eat. That danged horse wouldn't go more than a few steps with- out stopping for a snack. My youngest got a horse that was ready to RIDE, and it took off like the wind, with my littlest one hanging on for dear life until the wayward horse finally got the adrenalin out of his system. With the help of the lead trail rider, who managed to grab hold of the reins, my child was safely pulled in. By this time, I was getting pretty sure that horses were not "my cup of tea."

Several years later and right about the time that Mt. St. Helens was stirring up and ready to blow its top, one of our friends asked us if they could board their ancient Palomino barrel racing horse in our pasture and barn. What the heck? We thought having a horse to ride around on might be fun. So, every once in a while, I would saddle him up and try to take him for a ride. I might add he didn't think this was such a good idea. He was apparently tired of all the former racing in circles, crabbed and moaned that he was retired, and it wasn't his job to haul my big butt around when he should be just munching his way through the pasture. My husband finally hand-carved a stout wooden paddle and, in large red letters, painted "STOP" on one side and "GO" on the other as a present for me. Now, I had a little bit of an advantage over this lazy old horse, and with a few slaps of the paddle, I could finally get him to walk the length of the pasture and away from the barn. Upon turning around, all he could think of was getting to that barn as fast as he could and galloping like a bat out of hell on the return trip.

After this, I was about "done" with horses. They are pretty to look at, but I prefer four wheels to four sharp hooves, and I never did like the idea of possibly being a statistic. I also didn't want to take the risk of being thrown and suffering a brain injury or getting the snot pounded out of me by one or two of those flailing hooves, as deep down, my apprehension never let me entirely trust a horse.

Valerie Da Silva Curtiss

Chapter 11
Premarin Mare

Anthropomorphic writing is not my style, although it's all too precious and necessary in children's stories. I had a difficult time with it when I took the course, "Writing For Children." I struggled through and completed this course and found that I was lame in my attempt to write fiction. But if a mare could relate her suffering, it would absolutely break your heart, and I'm not going to make matters worse by giving these mares a "voice" in the following pages, although they very much need a voice, and one that can be heard loudly! The mares in this article are "Premarin Mares," mares whose urine is collected while pregnant so women can have "HRT" (hormone replacement therapy,) a miracle drug that keeps many of us from turning into "Screaming Meemies!," or being extremely impatient with our children, becoming overwhelmed with crying jags, hot flashes, and having a strong urge to kill our husbands...some of us had ended up in mental institutions like in days of old before doctors had some inkling of what women go through when hormones are depleted from the system. If you're old enough to recall the movie, "Snake Pit," you'll see what I'm speaking about in the actions of some of the women who were institutionalized. Big Pharma has quite the demand for this pregnant mare's urine-"PMU"-so this is about big bucks and pharmaceutical greed! I'm a darned hypocrite myself for writing an article like this because I've been on Premarin since the age of twenty-six after I had a total abdominal hysterectomy. All we had back then for estrogen was Premarin. I had no idea how a mare's urine was processed, and since I've had horses all of my life, I was purely happy to know that some part of the horse was inside me, no matter if it was pee! I try to lessen the guilt I now feel, after just recently learning how Premarin is processed, I also realize I am but a little mouse standing before the lion of the "Big Machine." My words are not going to put a halt to an industry so prolific and profitable, unless I am joined by the masses of women who now have high objection to the way mares are mistreated in order for this estrogen to be obtained.

I recently asked my doctor to decrease my dosage. This was a very small effort on my part, to save any one mare from the suffering she has to endure while the collection process goes on, it was also not as effective, and I began to feel symptoms of depletion. I tried many alternatives that just didn't work. The only thing I can do for these mares now is first, to pray for a solution to their suffering, and then attempt to enlighten any woman who reads this book. I hope she carefully researches this topic when she arrives at the point in her life should hormone replacement therapy be needed. In truth, I will tell you that going through hormone depletion was awful! I thought I was going insane. What happens to the "donating" mare, however, is abusive and very difficult to write about. Worse than this is the horror her foal faces, with many ending up dead, flattened like junk yard cars, and buried in a pit with so many others. Then there are foals sold to slaughterhouses, or brought into the industry to replace their exhausted dams, which makes more money through egregious suffering all the way 'round Some fortunate innocents are being rescued by as many people who can do this, and more rescue farms are now cropping up, they are very costly to run. Still, too many foals are lost in such a cruel, sad and very matter-of-factly way if you were to hear the words of some of the PMU farm managers, or those who send horses and foals to kill pens! It's purely business to them as usual and money doesn't just talk these days...it screams, and unfortunately, "It's all about money," in this world now.

By the year 2003, Manitoba, Saskatchewan and North Dakota held 400 farms that churned out gallon after gallon of pregnant mare's urine, to support the global HRT demand. Now, PMU farms are moving to China, Kazakhstan and Poland. Pfizer and Wyeth pharmaceutical companies continually pursue the HRT market as Premarin reaps bountiful monetary rewards and high profit margins. *Global sales were up 23% to the tune of $261 million in 2010, not increased by added prescriptions, but mainly coming from astronomically increasing prices, and also from non-prescription Internet sales. Currently, in North America, there are about forty farms with forty mares used on each.

The Collection Process

The mares typically used in these procedures of urine collection are the Draft breeds: The large Belgian, Clydesdale, Percheron and mixed-breed Quarter horses. There are other breeds used, but the bigger Draft horses are preferred for their abundance of urine output, and also for the higher concentration of hormones they possess. These mares are kept pregnant until they are no longer of use.

During the collection process, mares are tied to very small metal enclosures. There's no room for turning, lying down, going forward or backward. She just remains there, a slave to the industry. A rubber bag is placed under her tail to collect the urine. Worse, are the prolonged hours of standing in those little stalls, upwards of 10-12 hours a day, for most of her eleven month's pregnancy. She has very little time to be let out to run, graze, or lie down and rest. When her time is up and she can no longer produce, that's it! If there's no one to adopt her, or no rescue farm for her to go to, she's then taken to the slaughterhouse! An animal well knows the smell of blood. I can't begin to fathom the horror she senses, and the wails that come from her own kind going up that ramp ahead of her to be killed.

I'm devastated by the terror that fills this beautiful creature who has obediently stood by us, and who has served throughout the centuries as best friend, and as abused beasts of burden and war. Although the number of PMU farms has lessened in America, they still remain, and as we all know, "Big Pharma" is not going to stop any kind of lucrative business just for the "lowly" horse.

The down-side of estrogen use:

There is definitely a down-side to estrogen use. Contraindications show this medication is not just pure horse urine; it's synthesized, and other chemicals are added. Estrogen has been known to cause breast cancer, and increase the size of tumors already present in the body, and estrogen use can also increase your chances of stroke, heart attack and blood clots. If you're in need of HRT, please speak candidly with your prescribing doctor and check out other options. Bio-identical HRT works well for many and is plant-based. There is no generic form of Premarin, but a similar medication, a generic called Estradiol, that I tried caused my hair to fall out in alarming amounts! Dietary vigilance, the Vegan way, creams, low fats, exercises, etc., made no difference to me. I was experiencing hot flashes, and I'd cry at the slightest thing. I also angered quickly. In truth, hormone depletion can give you quite the "Jekyll and Hyde" syndrome! So, what role do I play in all of this? For now I can inform the readers. I can go on social media to hopefully enlighten the new generation of women out there, but for me, trying to go up against Big Pharma, as you well know, is completely impossible. At this time, Wyeth, a division of Pfizer, is facing more than 5000 personal injury lawsuits filed by women who took Prempro or Premarin. Prem Stoppers is a funding campaign for PMU mares, and is an organization who is trying to eliminate chemicals made from pregnant mare's urine. Do your research to see if there's anything you can do to help. The best thing I feel is spreading the word and sending money to rescue farms whose listings are readily available online.

Conclusion

I find myself between a rock and a hard place. I don't want any more mares to suffer because of me. In my case, without Premarin, I have no idea what would have happened to me with no treatment. I was twenty six years old when I had a total abdominal hysterectomy, and we had no information than, to let us know about the poor suffering mares. I doubt our doctors knew and we were just told to take it. It would be good for us. My bones remain strong, and I have no osteoporosis in spite of being post-menopausal and slight of stature. Other than age-related atherosclerosis and my spine being severely injured from accidents, I'm in general good health. I don't have heart problems or blood clots.

The PMU mare, however, is going to suffer nonetheless. Callous sounding? So very far from the truth! I don't know the why of all things; why so many good suffer, why so many bad do not! And like I said, I only very recently delved into the hormonal issue out of curiosity to see how it came to be Appalled? Yes! I was also very saddened, and then I became very angry at discovering how a poor mare is treated for the collection of her estrogen-rich urine. By the year 2017, no other hormone replacement therapy had come along to show me it was equal to Premarin, and I still have no solution for what I should try next. I will expect criticism for writing an article like this; I will "take my lumps," I don't back off easily, nor do I care what people may have to say or think about me. I'm plain dealing, and I am trying at the very least, to enlighten a new generation of women. For now, this is the only thing I can do. In many cases, it's been proved truthful that: "The pen is mightier than the sword." I happen to believe this adage. The quotation: "God blesses the beasts and the little children," I certainly hope rings true as well!

Lady Mo Pascoe-Hoyal

*Research: www.horsefund.org/pmu-fact-sheet-php

Facebook and Google searches also bring up many related articles under the search title:

"PMU MARES" or Premarin Mares.

APHE: Association of Professional Human Educators-Empathy through Education-online article and The National Humane Education Society also have articles online: (https://nhes.org)

Chapter 12
Fire Horse
Fiction based upon historical fact

Intro

World War 2 is well documented and much written about. However, horses played a very significant role in war-time, more than just for hauling soldier's ammunition. In 1941 the "National Fire Service" was created and expanded locally to include volunteers. Their equipment was often old and obsolete. Without these brave men and women, London, during the "Blitz," would have burned to the ground for all eternity. Mechanized fire trucks were the norm by the late 1930s, but river barges and old horse-drawn fire tenders were also used. Some horse-drawn fire tenders were even liberated from museums! This is a story in tribute to the brave men, women and horses, who gave their lives to keep London standing during the cataclysmic bombing raids of 1940 and 1941, termed "The London Blitz." Both my parents lived through these murderous times, and I feel all who fought to save London need mentioning.

Donald ran down the stairs and burst into the living room, "Slow down, Don, slow down," his mother said. Donald pulled on his dark blue uniform jacket which he wore with such pride. Grabbing a piece of bread from the old oak table he said, "Sorry Mum, I don't want to be late to the roll call. There may be another raid tonight." Laura shook her head and carried on knitting. Donald's father raised his eyes over the Evening Standard and said, "I'm finally proud of that boy. I knew he would come around once he left school at 14." Laura retorted, "Yes, I agree, but it's bloody dangerous what he does leading those horses into the fires."

It was common once dusk began to fall, to see men and women running for air-raid shelters or to the underground railway system. Donald ran as fast as he could and flew into the old fire station which had recently been opened, and its status as a museum put on hold. Five men stood in an informal line ready for inspection. Donald put on his heavy metal fire helmet and fell in line.

"Nice you could make it, Donald." Donald blushed and replied, "Sorry, Mr. Covington, the butcher kept me late cleaning the slabs down." Secretly, Mr. Covington was proud of Donald for keeping down a job and working seven nights a week in the "Auxiliary National Fire Service." After the parade, Donald walked out from the hall and into the cobbled stone back yard which housed the stables. A loud whinny broke the night sky as Rosie, the chest nut coloured mare threw her head up excitedly at seeing him. Being the youngest member of the group, Donald had been given the job of mucking out the stables and feeding the horses. He didn't mind spending time with Rosie.

"Are we going to be called tonight, Rosie?" The heavy-set mare raised her head from her feed bucket and nodded. Donald laughed and said, "I swear to God you understand what I'm saying!" Next he brushed Rosie down. He had remembered his talks with Mr. Covington about looking after the horses, and he took his job seriously for such a young man. Donald moved to the second stall and began grooming Violet. He looked after Violet just as well, but he had an unspoken affinity with Rosie, and everyone knew it.

Donald walked back into the musty fire station and joined the other volunteers with their cleaning and polishing of the old fire tender. Almost on queue the air raid siren shattered the night. It wailed and sent fear down the backs of any sane person. High above at 16,000 feet, Heinkel-111 German bombers droned overhead! Seen through the small fire station windows, people ran like the blazes to their designated air raid shelters. Surprisingly, there was no panic, just an orderly charge for shelter and sanctuary from the murderous bombing. Mr. Covington stood by the old Bakolite telephone and waited for the inevitable ringing. He snatched up the phone on the first ring. A hush fell over the room. He replaced the receiver, took a deep breath, and said, "Right, go!" It looks like St. Paul's is their target again. "Move!"

Donald ran outside and opened both Rosie's and Violet's stalls. He then opened the large dividing door between the yard and the main fire station. Rosie stood right behind Donald, her ears pricked forward as she listened to the incessant bangs and deep roars of the high explosives raining down on the London docklands. The bombing stream moved forward like an all-crushing giant. Windows erupted and broken glass spewed forth onto the scurrying people below.

Two minutes later the old fire tender emerged from the three-story building. Rosie and Violet were pulling the heavy, water-contained wagon through their thick leather harnesses. The volunteer firefighters ran by the side of the tender, there was no room for the men aboard. Donald ran by Rosie's side, holding the leather lead strap to her halter. The German bombers flew overhead with their engines deliberately un-synchronized. The volunteers ran hard and fast. Ahead, Donald could see the bright yellow glow of burning buildings. The night air became hot and acrid. Suddenly, the fire crew burst into a wall of searing heat! A huge twelve-story warehouse was in flames. Windows burst from the heat, sending glass raining down on the brave firefighters.

Donald looked at the myriad of snake-like hoses that littered the ground. At the end of each hose was a man directing water into the fire. A loud voice boomed from the shadows. "Get those horses out of the way, and you men start spraying my firefighters with water to stop them from burning up!"

A tall firefighter ordered the volunteers to action. Donald whispered to Rosie, "It's all going to be all right; you'll see." Donald was assuring himself more than Rosie, who never flinched as the explosions rocked the docklands. With the horses tied up to a broken roof beam, Donald began helping uncoil the heavy hoses. Next, an ancient steam engine slowly chugged into life, and a stream of water burst forth from the tender's hoses. Two men aimed the hoses at the downstairs window of the once proud fruit warehouse. The flames licked and roared in defiance of the cold water. Then a large hose was dragged between two rows of burning terraced houses. The tall firefighter shouted, "Hook that up to your engine. It's from the Thames fire boats."

With water from the River Thames filling the tender, the volunteer firefighters moved in closer to the creaking and crackling building. Donald stood wide-eyed and took in the horror of what stood before him. He felt an urge to do more than look after the horses, as much as he loved them, especially Rosie. He stroked her once more then ran to his crew mates. He saw Jim, the oldest of the volunteers, struggling to hold the hose against the enormous water pressure. Donald ran behind him and held some of the weight of the canvas hose. Jim immediately felt the hose be come lighter and looked behind him to see Donald holding the hose and staring at the flames. Minutes passed and the fire seemed to be abating. Overhead, another stream of German bombers lined up in formation over the burning docklands. It was their target. At 16,000 feet, Hans Lutz toggled the release switch to drop more high explosive and incendiary bombs from the aircraft.

Donald looked skywards as he heard a loud whistling noise. Then "karrump!" A 500 pound German bomb smashed through the burning roof of the warehouse and exploded on impact. The remaining windows blew out instantly. There was an audible creak and the upper part of the huge warehouse fell forward and out into the street! Donald saw this happening as if it were in slow motion. He tried to grab the older firefighter but the man had dropped to his knees and covered his face with his hands. Next, Donald found himself being lifted into the air and then slammed down hard onto the stone walkway.

The remaining firefighters ran across the street, away from the falling bricks and flames. After what seemed like an eternity, the smoke lifted, revealing a horrendous sight of broken brick and smoldering roof tiles. Mr. Covington looked to where his two crew members were standing. He began mumbling, "Oh Jesus, no. Jesus, no." The captain of the full time firefighters ran over to the safety of the standing houses and shouted to Mr. Covington, "Get your crew and those damned horses out of here. The bottom floors of the building could come down at any second!" Mr. Covington protested saying, "What about my men? One of them is only 14." The gruff and stressed-out fire captain shouted, "Get moving and take these horses. I won't tell you again! Your men are dead." With that he strode over to Rosie and grabbed her halter, and began tugging on it. Rosie reared up. Her eyes widened in panic and her pupils reflected the orange and red light emanating from the fires. Rosie's front hooves slammed down just inches from the captain. In terror, he ran backwards and tripped, caught himself just in time, and ran on shouting, "To hell with you lot then, you're on your own!"

Mr. Covington tried to calm Rosie, but it was too late. She had been watching Donald and she was insane with fear and anger. She reared again and the roof joist snapped in half with a resounding crack. Rosie bolted over to Donald. She whinnied and began pawing the bricks away from where he had stood. Rosie continued rearing up and smashing bricks under her hooves; sparks showered from her metal shoes. Mr. Covington felt helpless to save Rosie and knew better than to try to stop a horse when it was in full flight, mixed with fear and purpose. The warehouse swayed in the howling fire storm. The oxygen-fed fire shot flames higher into the night sky. Nothing could stop Rosie. She pawed and smashed her way into the pile of debris. Suddenly a white hand emerged from under the rubble. Rosie whinnied even louder. She lowered her head and laid her reins onto the hand. The hand didn't move. Rosie whinnied and stomped the bricks again. As if by miracle the hand grabbed the leather rein. Rosie very gently moved backwards, and the handheld its grip. Slowly an arm emerged from the rubble, then a shoulder, and with one almighty pull from Rosie, Donald came out from the fiery pit!

The firefighters' jaw dropped open. Mr. Covington said, "I don't believe it. I've never seen anything like this in all my life." Donald coughed and gasped at what air he could. His colleagues carried him around the block into cooler air. Donald gulped water from a canteen. He opened his eyes and said, "Where's Rosie? Is she okay? She saved me." Rosie and Violet were led around the block and into safety. Mr. Covington said, "There she is, lad. She's okay." Rosie nuzzled Donald as he lay on the canvas stretcher. Donald stroked her head and said, "Thank you, old girl. You saved me." Donald drifted off into semi-consciousness. He heard the ambulance bells clanging as Rosie whinnied in triumph!

Lord David L. Banks

Chapter 13
My Stubborn Thing

Children don't always take after their parents when it comes to the love of animals, mine sure didn't! Oh, once in a while they may have had a dog or would feed a stray cat, but neither of my children have displayed my long kinship with animals even though they were raised with many. They aren't much for gardening either. After all of this time I found out the other day while on the phone with my daughter that she says I have a stubborn thing. This "stubborn thing" is for my continuance in horse ownership. Apparently, this is what she has thought...for years. I'm 75 this year, I've had my mare for over eleven years, a sweet pony for almost seven, besides having horses for nearly most of my life. It is costly and the work has now become too much for me. I'm waiting for a second go-round, to try a more superior spinal cord neuro stimulator that would hopefully enable me to do all of my barn and house chores again. Any riding may be out of the question, but I'd just love to get on my horse-by way of forklift-and ride her calmly around at a safe pace. Someone would have to go with me and that's a whole other thing. The Queen in England has her outrider, still rides at ninetyone, but we were born in very different galaxies, you can be sure. All I have to say about this stubborn thing of mine, is you don't have a horse, love her, train her and ride for years, each one loving and trusting the other, only to discard her like an old shoe. Perhaps I should have asked my daughter which of her three children did she want to give away? I don't know if this would get through as my children don't think horses would be a real part of the family. How could these two aliens- non-animal loving creatures have ever been born to me? I'll never understand. They had to get these genes from their Dad or from some distant family DNA? But when I'm at a fork in the road, the sign post with the horse on it will always be my choice to go down. I don't ask my children for help, so what's the beef? I think they mainly feel this way because I have endured a very unhappy marriage of 32 years, living with an abusive alcoholic who continues to make my life miserable. Both children have always expressed their desire for me to get out of this toxic relationship, but my only choices so far, are to sell my horse and pony, move to a government-subsidized apartment where the four white walls in a very tiny, noisy place would come crashing in on me. Also to be considered are the costs for electricity, food, medication, auto upkeep, monthly bills and medical insurance that I'd have to pay from a not-so-hefty Social Security check. I'd never make it even with reduced rent. My sister has kindly offered a place for me in her loving home, but I would never be able to move my little kingdom into one bedroom. In spite of my unhappiness at home, I at least bought the land outright with my own money. However, we are in a community property state, so I'd most likely have to split the sale. I call this my little postage-stamp farm. I have yards, gardens, lots of space, a henhouse, and I've been safe here for twenty-seven years. This little homestead's paid off, and besides, I'm not going to let anyone ride roughshod over me, drive me out, so I lose my part of this investment, which over the years has added up to a considerable sum. I'll put up with the stupid drunk, keep praying and continue buying a few lottery tickets...people win every day, so why not me? I'll keep my horses and some semblance of a life I've been trying to have for years. I'm blessed in being able to still hobble out the back door and have my horse family happily running up to me, whinnying for a kiss and a treat. I can still feed them, and to me, this is a big deal. My mare and pony are very much a large part of my heart and happiness. You just can't take the horse out of this woman...this woman who's loved the horse ever since she was a wee girl, we're born with it. No one's allowed to say anything about my having horses; this is my territory. You can't enter into this decision, and I've never asked for your opinion. This goes for my husband as well. I've worked hard all of my life, always earned my own way and got what I wanted or needed until I became disabled. I still pay my own way and for my horses. So, kids, talk about something else besides mama's "stubborn thing!" I don't want to live with either one of you anyway. When comes the time I can't navigate, just put me in a nursing home where I can tape horse pictures to the walls and drive the nurses and administration batty with them. When I know my "goose is cooked" for horse keeping, I'll be the first one to make this judgment. I'll sadly give my horse and pony to a nice family, one who'd want a gentle, devoted but aged mare and a sweet children's pony, still very much ride-worthy. I'll let their tack go with them and throw in my good tandem horse trailer. So far, there are no signs of dementia, although I won't deny a few "senior moments" here and there. When I do go down, you can bet it will be with both guns blazing!

What causes people to be kindred, or to have an affinity with something or another, like animals, hair-raising sports, gambling, drugs, alcohol, writing, music, the daily walk and all else that people do and love in habitual ways? I believe it's in our composition, our DNA, and that we're predisposed to one thing or another. I'm just so thankful I wasn't born with the craving to drink or gamble. My addiction remains the horse; I can't help it. It's there, always has been, and always will be. I've tried to make it go away, smashed thoughts and desires and was without a horse for thirty years. Later on, when I got to this little place, the "craving" started back up. I knew our land could hold a horse, and so I began working slowly toward this goal. After all, I prayed all those thirty years to have just one more horse before I died. I worked my last job at age sixty-seven and paid for the set-up myself: my little barn and feed room, all fencing, gates, tack for ridding, grooming implements, I got a loan for my truck after selling my small Ford Mustang, and also bought a very good tandem horse trailer for a song...all used but in very good condition. I then went about my business. I briefly had one other horse before settling on this mare and added a beautiful Palomino Welsh pony for my grandson, who, after three months of training, decided horses weren't his thing. Now, this lovely pony is a barn buddy and can still serve a purpose by annoying my mare while keeping her on her toes and her blood flowing nicely. Does anyone understand yet?

So we wait...my mare, my pony and me, for the outcome of my success with yet another spinal neurostimulator. If this one fares much better than the first one that only worked while it was outside of my body during the nine-day trail, perhaps I can at least achieve some simple goals I've set aside for myself. I want to be able to muck out my own stall and paddock, groom my horses better, bend to clean out hooves, walk without agonizing pain, get house chores done, and see if who offered to take me on gentle rides is still up for it. If I could ride just twice a month along a safe trail or in an open meadow, I think I'd be about the happiest person one could ever see. I still possess good hands and a seat. Riding would also be wonderful for my mare, who I know misses me very much. It would help us both tremendously. There'll be no "hell bent for leather" anymore; it's not what I now desire...oh, maybe to jump over a wee tree that's fallen to the ground or go a short canter. I miss my mare's funny habit of kicking up both back legs if she gets the crop to her rump, which is rare. It's HER stubborn thing. I'd just love an over-all safe ride now instead. I think this would find me better able to withstand the "Tempest in the tea pot" that I'd always come home to. Being able to ride again would greatly fortify me in strength of muscle and soul, while adding hope and giving me something to look forward to. Very bleak have been my days of late, and when I see women still riding through their eighties and nineties, I'm just a young un compared to them. You can't take the horse out of me. It IS and will always remain a large part of my soul.

As an afterthought, there is no anger or aggravation directed at my children; they're just not me. They don't feel as I do; I never forced it upon them, which I can fully understand. What I do not get is when I'm told I have a stubborn thing. Let me be! My life is going to work out as it's supposed to, according to "someone higher up" who has a plan for each and every one of us. For now, I can't bear to part with either horse or pony who gives me the will to keep going. If things should become dire, I have sense enough to know when my "goose is cooked." I always pray that I can place my babies with a good family who will love them and be kind to them, a family who will keep them together. In the meantime, leave me be! I can't take the nasty alcoholic moods in this house, but a trip out the back door to see my beloveds quickly dispels anything that burdens my heart as soon as these devoted equines run up to me like innocent little children. Sweet, loving "children" that I simply cannot give away...just yet.

Mosie Appleseed

Chapter 14
The Magic Can Come Back!

I've loved horses all of my life. I'm 64 now and still going strong! As a young girl, I had statues of horses in my bedroom and surrounded myself with what I thought was the most beautiful creature in the universe. I still feel this way. I was so in love with horses and would wake up early on Saturday mornings to catch the Roy Rogers show just to look at his beautiful Palomino, Trigger. I'd watch any cowboy show I could, just to see the horses in them: "The Lone Ranger," "My Friend Flicka," or "The Cisco Kid." I didn't care what the story was about or who the performers were. I had dreams of owning a beautiful Palomino and can't tell you how I begged my parents to buy me a horse, but we lived in the city and that was just out of the question.

My family owned a summer home in Waveland, Mississippi and every summer when school let out, my mother would pack up my siblings and me, and we'd spend the entire season in Mississippi. My cousins had found a ranch that rented horses for an hourly ride, and we talked our parents into letting us go there to ride now and then. It was the highlight of my summer, being on the back of one of those horses. I remember to this day, the name of the horse I always asked for; his name was Pepper. He was a gray gelding and how I loved seeing him.

One summer, a very big surprise came my way. My aunt and uncle would come to spend time at our summer home. They knew how much I loved horses. My uncle had a friend who lived in Waveland, who in turn had a daughter who had a horse by the name of Buddy, a Palomino by the way. My uncle's friend told him his daughter had to attend summer school for eight weeks. Since it was a boarding school it meant she wouldn't be home for eight weeks. My uncle's friend asked if I'd be interested in keeping the horse for that period of time, to care for and to and ride him. You see, our summer home was on about five acres so I was able to keep him like he was my very own. It was heaven for those eight wonderful weeks. I rode, groomed and fed him and pretended he was my very own. The next year the same offer was made and Oh, what a wonderful and magical summer that was again with "my" Buddy! When the following year rolled around I wasn't able to get buddy because his owner didn't have to attend summer school, and of course, she wanted her horse, much to my extreme disappointment. I was so very down that my parents found another place that rented horses. They let me go now and then, but the horses at this stable were not as friendly as I had been accustomed to and they would try to rub my legs on fences, run me into trees, and even turn their heads and try to bite while I was riding. I didn't understand back then, but the reason they behaved this way was that they were not always treated kindly by the riders who rented them, and it was a self-defense retaliation on their part. It didn't bother me, though, I was on a horse! All through my life I rode any horse I could if the situation presented itself. Whatever opportunity came along, I grabbed that brass ring!

When I was older and got married, I moved to north Texas with my husband where we had purchased several acres in the country. We were outside one day looking down our pasture and I made the comment that a beautiful Palomino would look great in there. My husband told me, "Why don't you go buy one?" So I started looking around the very next day. I found a beautiful white, five year old horse that was for sale. The owner informed me that he was a Tennessee Walking Horse. I had no idea what a Tennessee Walking Horse was and bought him just the same. His name was Slick. I rode him almost every day. I groomed him every day. I loved him every day. We rode so much over the years that we knew what the other was thinking. We were so connected.

In 2006 my husband died of a brain aneurysm. Eventually I moved back to Louisiana and made plans for Slick to come with me. I resided in Opelousas and Slick was staying on a friend's farm close by. I lived there for one and a half years and then moved to New Orleans for a job opportunity. Slick had to stay in Opelousas, but I traveled every weekend to be with him. By this time, we had been together for about fourteen years.

After some time I met someone else and married. My new husband was offered a job in Opelousas where my beautiful boy was being stabled and we found a place in the country with a pasture to lease, so we moved there with Slick in tow.

My husband, David, also had a horse. We rode together and it was a wonderful life with my new husband and my special boy. About six months after we were married David found out he had stage four cancer and the treatments began, so did the expenses. After about a year, I made the difficult and heartbreaking decision to find homes for our horses because the future was so uncertain. A woman in Texas took my sweet baby boy, and my heart was broken. After sixteen years together, he was going to be away from me forever. To this day I will never forget the way he looked at me when I left him... he knew. I still live with that picture in my mind, of him turning his head and just looking at me walking away from him. At one point I tried to get him back, but the people who had him wouldn't part with him. My heart still aches for him to this day. After about a year of cancer treatment, my wonderful husband started to feel better and knew how much I missed my horse. He contacted Camelot Wilderness Ranch in Leonville, LA, where they breed and raise Tennessee Walking Horses. David arranged for us to go out there to look at some of the horses that were for sale (because, you see, he also missed our horses.) We bought two that day, Smokey and Magic. Smokey was to be my horse, and Magic was for David. We kept them at the ranch and often rode together and sometimes just went there to groom them or sit and watch them graze. We had those babies for about two years until my husband's cancer came back with a vengeance. It took his life in November of 2013.

While David was in the hospital, I hadn't seen Smokey and Magic for about four weeks, but Ginger, the ranch owner, was taking very good care of them. After David died, my heart was bro- ken into so many pieces I could hardly stand it. I couldn't bring myself to do anything that David and I used to do together, and I couldn't bear to go to the ranch where the horses were. David and I had spent so many wonderful times together out there. Also, it had changed my financial situation drastically! I asked the couple who owned the ranch (who had now become friends) to find homes for the horses because I didn't think I could ever go back to the ranch again and didn't yet know what I could afford. They agreed to take them back and find new homes for them. Five months went by and I heard that Smokey went to live in Texas with a good owner. Magic actually stayed at the ranch and now belonged to Lacey, a young woman whom I had ridden with on many occasions.

During these black days, I felt there was nothing left to live for without my best friend. I had also lost my mother the same year. I was now living in a place where I had no family. To make a long story short, I went to visit Ginger and told her that I was so sad and thought I needed to be around horses again. She told me if I could get myself back to the ranch, she'd let me use one of her horses as though it was mine. I convinced myself to return to the ranch and Ginger let me use Lady. Lady helped me heal! Taking care of her and riding her was far better therapy than any psychotherapist could have ever given. Little by little, I finally started feeling alive again.

After several trips back to the ranch, Lacey, the young woman who had my husband's former horse, Magic, was also keeping her there. Magic and Lady were in the same pasture! The first day I walked into the pasture to catch Lady, Magic walked up to me and put her head right into my chest as if she was giving me a hug. Remember, she used to be David's horse, and her contact made me feel as if David was still with me. But she was now someone else's horse, so there wasn't much I could do. I also had another dilemma; there was definitely something between Magic and me.

As the months went by Lacey saw how Magic responded to my presence. One day, she gave her back to me and told me it was because she knew that Magic and I belonged with each other. Magic and I have been together for almost a year now and I will do everything in my power to keep her. I ride her almost every day. I groom her every day. I love her every day. She is now the love of my life. Lady brought me back to life...but Magic breathes exuberance into me. In return, I give her my unending love and appreciation.

Dale Raccuglia

Chapter 15
Safety Along The Trail

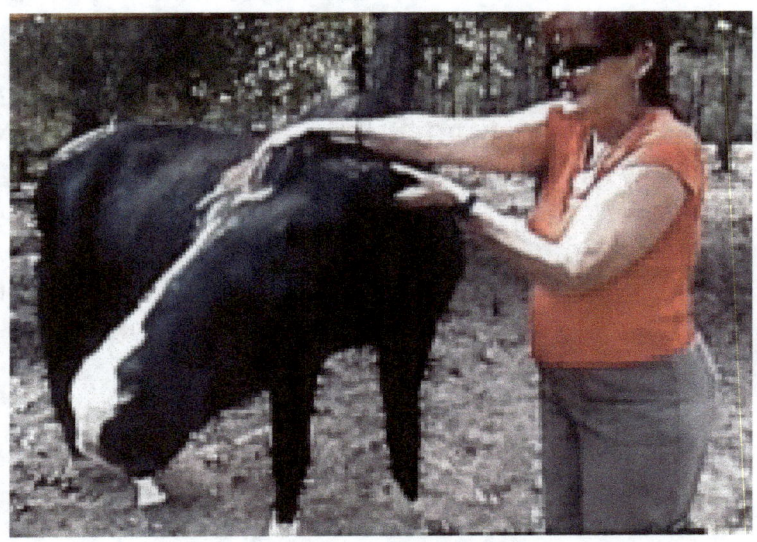

Trail riding has always been an enjoyable way to spend special times with my horse. I can think of no other activity I'd prefer doing. Trail riding can also be beneficial for both horse and rider. There's no competitive pressure that is demanded from the show ring, or what arena events require. In riding trails, you can spend as much or as little time as you feel both you and your horse can tolerate. When I go for a trail ride, I prefer some of that time to be spent taking photos along the way, and don't push my horse to go "hell bent for leather." Some riders enjoy faster-paced rides, but I sometimes like to dawdle whenever I want to and since my mare's name is Lolly, there are moments when we just love to lollygag along. Actually, Lolly was the name I chose for my mare, especially because her gentle way is reminiscent of a couple of cartoon characters with their remarks of,

"Do, de, oh", or "I'm bringing home a baby bumblebee, won't my mommy be so proud of me."

Although trail riding is a great way to spend time with your horse, there are also safety issues and possible pitfalls along the way. Having a plan for protection is a good thing to procure. I've been on some rides when immature persons acted with "Tom Foolery" and caused a lot of problems for other riders, to include a girl on a borrowed horse that stopped so fast and hard it threw her off, rendering her unconscious! Not being familiar with her mount and not realizing how fast this horse could stop, the fractious riders ahead of her stopped too quickly for the speed they were going and off she went. This ride could have possibly ended in tragedy. Sometime after this incident, a group of teenagers on a ride came upon a wire about one foot off the ground. They took for granted it wasn't a hot power line. The first rider's horse cleared it when coached to jump. The second rider's horse became very nervous-and darn it- this should have been taken as a warning sign of the animal sensing better than its rider, but by obeying its master, they both got caught up in it, and both were electrocuted. Horse and rider died on the scene! It was noted the other riders observed how nervous the second horse had become when approaching the wire, which only goes to confirm further, that the horse felt danger when the rider did not. Trying to prove how brave you are and how you can ride like the dickens is not good riding or good judgment in my opinion. All wires on the ground MUST be taken as live wires, please! The unnecessary death of this young man and his horse rocked our community for quite some time and has left a very indelible mark upon us all.

Before going on any ride, there are things you should do and look for. Beginning with your horse and gear. Check your animal for any cuts or abrasions that may not be healed properly enough to allow your horse to go safely on the ride. These injured spots can worsen and even become infected by some of the rigors that can occur during the ride.

Pick your horses's hooves clean, and make sure to include the hoof pick in your horn or saddle bags. Check all tack curb chains/straps, and always take your halter and lead rope with you, tied to your saddle. Never think anything is ideal, this isn't the way of life, or at least it's not happening in mine!

Know your riding area. During the ride, be aware of rotted-out trees that leave dangerous holes in their stead. Some of these holes can be difficult to see if covered with grass and a horse can break its leg going in and trying to come out of one. Watch for fallen trees with circumferences too large for your horse to clear when attempting to jump over them. There are many other things along the route to be watchful for besides holes. Branches can be too low, ground is boggy, a trail too narrow, rotted boards on wooden bridges that carry you over terrain or water, snakes in creeks (a good pair of polarized sun glasses helps you to see a snake in a creek or shallow stream, trust me.) There can also be countless other hazzards too numerous to list for now.

While on a ride one lovely day, there happened to be two large buzzards feasting on carrion just ahead of us on the trail. With our horses approaching, the huge birds with wide-spanning wings quickly took off, leaving us all with our horses spinning, snorting, prancing and some turning inside-out! You never know that lies ahead and a horse may spook when it sees or smells deer, hogs, hunters, loud four-wheelers, or maybe even Bigfoot! Never take one thing for granted and don't be so relaxed that you become limp as a dishrag or ride with one leg slung over the saddle horn as we may often do to give relief to a sore limb. Be alert at all times, look above and below you, from side-to-side...and be a defensive rider. Never think your horse is so "bomb proof" that you'll be totally safe. Keep in mind when a horse becomes frightened enough, it will run off and very well may leave you in the dirt behind him. Horses are creatures of flight when they become frightened enough. I haven't seen much horse loyalty in my many years of riding where a horse is so concerned for its owner that it sticks around to make sure no harm comes to them. Most of that noble behavior is Hollywood's depiction of how we'd love it to be, for example: "My Friend Flicka," "Gallant Bess," or "The Black Stallion."

When the ride has been completed, please ensure your horse is calmed down and properly cooled off before loading it into the trailer. I've seen riders run all the way back to their parked trailers and load their blowing and dripping wet horses, only to let them cool off on the way home. No, no, no! I witnessed a beautiful young gaited horse contract pneumonia from this very action, and he had to be hospitalized, causing much anguish to his owner, not to speak of a very expensive Veterinary bill in the curative treatment.

Listed below are some useful items to bring along on a ride, no matter how brief the ride may be: Bottled water, a ration of grain for your horse, energy bars for you, a hoof pick, a utility knife, duct tape which has many uses-even for bandaging, cigarette lighter, Band-Aids, Ace bandage that can be used for horse and human. Keep a pen and paper with your name, address, phone number, and a contact name and number should anything happen to you. Carry a thin rain parka, space blanket, a whistle, cell phone and hand sanitizer. Believe it or not, just about all of these items fit very nicely into a horn bag. For more or larger items, the use of saddle bags gives you more space.

Some other precautions to take: Don't follow nose-to- tail on a ride. You won't be able to see where your horse is going, and neither will your horse. Also, a lot of horses won't put up with an unfamiliar one coming up so close to its hindquarters, my mare won't! Don't permit your horse to run downhill, nibble at grass or leaves along the way, and don't ride farther or longer than you or your horse's tolerance allows. If training your horse along the trail take last position, please! There's nothing more annoying than to be behind a horse when its rider makes frequent stops or turns. The constant stopping to correct is very inconsiderate and downright rude! Men, please act like gentlemen. Women forget the chatty gossip; some people just like the sounds of the woods and creeks along the way. Friendly banter at quick stops is fine.

Nothing can be more fulfilling than to spend quality time with your horse. If you have some trusted buddies to go along, this is a big plus. Trail riding is good for mind, body and soul. It gets you out of yourself and your worries frees up stress and eliminates the humdrum of every day life.

If I were asked what my religious preference is, I'd have to say that, "I am an Equestropalian. My Cathedral lies under a canopy of trees!" "Happy trails to you," and may your trails always be safe to traverse. (Quote credit: Lisa Bryant-Lady Mo Pascoe-Hoyal)

Lady Mo Pascoe-Hoyal

Photo Credit:

Wayne E. Hoyal

Chapter 16
Amber Green Eyes

(Her Legacy, July 5, 2001 to December 16, 2015)

I was first introduced to horses through a couple of ponies named Ball, a small Shetland; my memory of him is only from pictures, and I eventually graduated to Skipper, a Welsh pony that my grandparents purchased for my cousins and me. Those youthful experiences helped me to acquire the skill of assertiveness, as ponies tend to be Napoleonic. If I wanted to ride, I had no choice but to learn on them. On Skipper's back in my pretend world as a child, I was a beautiful princess with the wind blowing through my hair as I rode on the back of a handsome steed, playfully weaving in and out of trees and of course, trying not to get rubbed off along the way. I ignored those incidents, and like any princess, I lifted my head high and looked straight ahead, undaunted as I rode along. As my confidence grew on the back on that little Welsh pony, so did my skill level. I began to make him rear up, like Silver did on "The Lone Ranger" television show. I was incessantly getting into trouble for "herding" the cattle. That little pony and I had a lot of fun together, but all things have an ending. I grew up, and Skipper was eventually sold. It wasn't until many years later that I had the opportunity to yet again, have a horse back in my life, a Tennessee Walking horse, who happened to be a stallion. I saved him from an auction house, ready for slaughter. Though our time together was very short, only a few months, he was a dream to ride. He had stolen my heart, and he took great care of me. He apparently knew nothing about "stallions being problematic to handle," and neither did I. I lost him to strangles, an equine illness, a short time later, but he made me fall in love with the Tennessee

Walking Horse breed. I decided I wanted to become a breeder. I read everything I could, talked to all the experts, made trips all over the place, and I learned "by fire!" I then purchased my prized stallion, Color Quest T.F., whose eyes were baby blue, and I began to add to my little herd little by little. Those years were some of the most joyful of my life. As time went on, I ended up with two stallions who were both big Teddy Bears whom I both bred and rode, and Ah, the joys of new life...as the foals started to come. To me, foals are one of the most enduring creatures on earth. Early on, I was going through the mare selection process up in middle Tennessee when I spotted a seven-month old champagne filly who was dragging her handler behind her. In fact, he was skiing along grass. I laughed. She was huge and had sea-green eyes. As I watched her, I felt particularly drawn to this filly...way too young for my breeding program and way too pricey as a young horse with obviously no training in manners whatsoever. Yet, I "felt" her. She was to be my horse, not a brood mare, just my horse. As I sat there watching, I knew in my heart and soul she would be worth the wait. I signed on the dotted line and brought her home with me.

Ginger Otzenberger Schouest and Amber Green Eyes

Amber became her name, and just as I did with my ponies, we sort of grew up together; she was in age, and I in learning about raising a young horse and turning her into a multi-purposed one. In the beginning, I just interacted with her pretty much as I did with my pony, Skipper. At that point in time, that's all I had as my basic "horse training" knowledge and I began to relive those child- hood experiences on some level. Amber and I just "did" things together because I didn't know how to professionally train her. I laughed at her, at the things she would so, and the mistakes we both made. Fortunately, rubbing me off against trees didn't seem to be of any interest to her. We just had fun. Our trust in one another grew in leaps and bounds, as did our bond. Over the years the communication between us began to change into something much more. A slight look or a movement, and we understood one another. As time went on, I began to feel intuition whenever I was with Amber. Words in my head felt like strong feelings. A great example would be when I bred Amber. To me, she was so perfect that I wanted another one just like her, and I sensed from her that she wanted a foal. I came home from work one day with an overwhelming feeling that Amber was going to a foal that evening. It was two weeks early. I went out and bathed her and got her ready. My husband joined me and noticed none of the tell-tale signs of pending delivery. He didn't believe me, although I remained steadfast in my knowledge. I stalled Amber for the evening and kept returning to her. At about midnight, I broke down and cried in her stall from the anxiety. I was worried about her. My sweet Amber gently nudged me into the corner and wrapped her head around me, giving me a gentle but firm horse hug. In my head, I heard, ' It will all be okay." I asked from my heart, "What time shall I return then?" I heard "5:00 a.m." I accepted her thoughts, wiped my tears, and went back in to set my clock.

The alarm went off precisely at that time. I got up, pulled on my boots, grabbed a robe and flashlight as it was still dark out, and made my way to the barn. I flicked on the light and smiled. Still in the sack, with steam coming off his little body, was a beautiful colt who looked just like Amber; in fact, it looked like she had cloned herself. Had I set the clock five minutes earlier, I would have witnessed the actual birth. I knew then I could "hear" Amber. She taught me how to listen, how to communicate beyond words and body language, and how to trust that feeling of "knowing" with that experience. With Amber, it was overwhelmingly easy. She had such a big presence and her energy just seemed to somehow open that door for me.

Sometime later, I decided to take classes to improve my skills as a horsewoman. During that time, I lost touch with some of those "listening" skills as I focused more on the proper way of doing things, especially around my peers. My "hearing" abilities waxed and waned. Amber had a way of teaching me when I wasn't listening. She literally wouldn't commune with me for weeks at a time. She'd walk away from me when I entered her pasture and would stand at a distance, just looking at me. When we were on track, this never occurred. There were many tearful moments when she brought me to my knees. I always told others our relationship...was complicated. But, relationships also become greater in depth as they make us look more clearly into our own hearts and souls. They help us to personally grow and then hopefully grow together, that is, if we are willing to hear one another and learn from our mistakes. If we can and do, the bonding becomes more concrete. And yet, another life lesson from Amber. I use that lesson learned, that wisdom she imparted, with humans in my life now.

I began to know Amber was wise....a Sage. She was not just a teacher of humans but of the herd out here as well. Many witnessed her breaking up horse fights with just her presence and a look or taking her position as lead mare without ever harming new horses. We watched as she did those dances with the tougher ones, all the while looking back at us to make sure we saw and understood. We would watch, mesmerized. Such a beautiful, graceful dance. We could see the pride in her eyes as she searched for the pride in ours. She did the same with us, just in a different way. Amber and I would often meditate together, she would hover over me. These were some of the most peaceful moments of my life, being surrounded by her sweet energy. On one occasion, I experienced a most profound feeling...as she looked deeply into my eyes. I felt a tingling sensation up and down my spine and a fluttering in my heart. It felt as though she was looking deep inside, seeing my soul. That was the "feeling or knowing." It literally took my breath away. Our relationship soared to a new height after that.

I decided to do a test one day. I knew I had learned to "hear" Amber, though I didn't always listen or couldn't understand her clearly. I wanted to see if she could "hear" me, and I tested this by lunging her in the round pen. As she was going around, I purposely did not change my body language and didn't move. I sent out a thought.... Whoa! She stopped dead in her tracks and turned to look at me. She could "hear" me too! I used this on a trail ride up in the mountains of Oklahoma some time later. My husband was confused as to which way to take back to camp though he didn't want to admit it, and daylight was fading. Amber was sending me messages, "wrong way, wrong way," which I told my husband. At first, he refused to listen. We just rode on. Finally, he gave in. I communicated to Amber, "take us home," and gave her the lead. Off we went down the mountainside, a trail we'd never ridden on, and mountains in which we'd never been. Once again, I "knew" we were heading back to camp. My horse had this. It turned out to be a short cut, in fact, because we were back at camp in no time. From that day forward, my husband listened to Amber and me without hesitation.

The years flew by, and I watched Amber's dances while stealing moments with her as I lived my busy life, thinking we had many years left, along with many more happy times. I wish I had stolen more time. In 2014, Amber's back leg swelled up like a stovepipe. That's what the condition is called, a "stovepipe leg." She spent a week with the Vet. No good answers were forthcoming. She eventually returned to normal, but I kept feeling it was her lymph nodes. In the summer of 2015, there were more strange health issues. Vets found a large mass next to major arteries internally, but since there are no definitive tests for cancer in equines other than melanomas, the diagnosis was only speculative. I was to bring her back in a few months to see if the mass had grown.

If it was cancer, it would be inoperable due to its location, just too close to major arteries. We'd know if it was cancer by continued growth. All health issues, however, seemed to disappear by fall, so I hoped for the best.

In November of 2015, we went on our first cattle roundup. Amber was a natural. We rode together as a team, with mostly her as Captain. (I had to draw on my earlier childhood experiences which were limited to that of child's play.) Our first encounter with a wayward cow gave me clue #1 that the weekend was going to prove to be much more than what would meet the eye. As the cow broke loose from the heard, Amber and I moved to cut it off. I turned her in the direction the cow was running, but Amber made an executive decision to side pass instead, all the while maintaining eye contact with the cow. This enabled us quick maneuverability if the cow changed direction. I understood that after the fact. The cow reached us, stopped, mooed, shook its head in protest, then turned around and ran back to the herd. My horse was steadfast, her gaze never faltering. I sat there in shock. Whatever she had communicated, it was obvious that the cow took her seriously. The next day, we had yet another mystifying experience. We had an opportunity to cut a calf from a herd, another first for us both. The goal was to single out the horned calves from the non-horned. We joined the riders lined up to do it and waited our turn, watching all the while. Finally, our moment came. We moved out of the line-up, and I simply picked a calf with horns, with my eyes and my mind, from a group of thirty or forty. He was right in the middle of them. We moved toward that group of calves and somehow, my horse just knew. We quickly managed to get that calf and five others away from the group and then separated the other four from him while he exited the pen. It took only about five minutes. I was using my English saddle, and all I remember doing was keeping my eyes on that calf. Amber, as far as I can recall, did everything else. It was surreal. Afterward, I sat there stunned, asking myself how we had just done that. My brain had a hard time processing this. I certainly had NO experience doing this kind of work and neither had my horse. How did she know which calf? I wondered why I felt no movement in my saddle. Surely we moved in a myriad ways to keep that calf from rejoining its group. It all happened so fast, so efficiently, so smoothly, I just couldn't grasp it. It was as if Amber and I were one in those few moments. That is the only way I can describe it. She knew my thoughts and kept me firmly and securely seated in that English saddle no matter which way she moved. We executed our most perfect dance together as one. I didn't need a western saddle with a horn as cutters use, and Amber needed no training to cut calves from a herd. We just did it. Just as it was with my pony, Skipper, and Amber in our early days. What a gift my horse gave me! Sadly, that very special ride was to be our last. A few weeks later, I was to say goodbye to my best friend, my spiritual teacher, and the love of my life. She ate her supper that last night, and everything appeared to be in order. In the early morning light of the following day we found Amber's herd standing around her lifeless body. The discovery of that loss was deafening. The "knowing," profound. My world fell flat that day; all the color, gone. I felt lifeless as well.

As I look back in honoring her memory, in some ways, my life came full circle that weekend as I rode my Amber, herding those cattle just as I had done in my youth on my pony, Skipper. Amber gave me the greatest of last rides here on earth. Amber drove home what she had been teaching me all along with that ride; that there is more beyond what we experience with our five senses. I hold onto that, to that ride, to those lessons...and look forward to the time I can sit on her glorious back once more. I choose to honor her by working on developing those gifts and insights she showed me. We are all sentient beings. We must open our hearts and minds to hear one another. And then we must learn to listen. I search for Amber's ability to communicate through to other horses, or in the gentle breezes that sweep the hair from my face as I ride and look for her in the stars and heavens. I "know" she is there. I am thankful to God for the many blessings he gave me by allowing Amber Green Eyes to be a part of my life for fourteen years and, most of all...for allowing my soul to intimately bond with the soul of one of His very special "Earth Angels."

Ginger Otzenberger-Schouest

Photo Credit:

Mo Pascoe –Hoyal

Chapter 17
Toxic Plants... To Horses And Humans

What prompted me to write this article was hearing news some years ago about a horse in California who ingested just seven leaves of the Oleander bush and nearly died. This lethal plant is attractive in fragrance and smells like something that came from a bakery. The suffering anguish really, that comes to the animal is worse than painful, and if the animal heals, it can be a long and expensive process, with damage done, and often times, the animal dies in spite of it. As a young girl in Hawai'i, a family of tourists held a picnic at one of our scenic beaches. They unknowingly used sticks from branches of the Oleander to roast their hot dogs with. All of this dear family died.

From its fragrance, I can see why a horse would be drawn to it, as I always imagined cupcakes and icing every time I took a whiff of its enticing fragrance. Fortunately, we were taught early on about this beautifully malicious plant! Those of us who love our horses need to take great measures in ensuring their safety, and to have at least a bare bones knowledge of what grows in our areas that may be poisonous to animals and to humans as well.

While researching poisonous botanicals, I was shocked to learn how many of them contain enough toxins to kill such a large and powerful animal as the horse. Also, I wasn t aware of what grew in my neck of the woods, some right here in my yard. As if things couldn't get any worse, there are countless others that are lethal, and we may not know about. Some toxic plants are so noxious that the agony suffered before a horse succumbs to death can only be described as horrid! You'd be fortunate if your Veterinarian could save your horse, but the medical costs for this kind of treatment would probably be astronomical. Please keep in mind, that the listings below are only a general accounting, and the list is not complete. It would benefit you to do your own research for your area. Be careful where you let your horse graze; never let them yank leaves from trees and bushes while on a ride.

An abridged list of toxic plants, shrubs, and flowers: * indicates deadly poison

Azalea/rhododendron-avocado

Black locust, black walnut/blue periwinkle-Vince

Bracken fern- buttercups

Cape tulip-cape week-*castor bean-plant. Its seeds contain ricin

Choke berry-cockle burr-Cook Town Ironwood- camera

Daffodil-dandelion, Darling, *deadly nightshade-all Angel trumpet family

Field wort-flat weed-*foxglove

Green Cestrum-Groundsel-Guildford grass

*Hemlock-horse tail

Johnson grass

Lantana-leafy spurge-locoweed-lupin

Mother of millions-mountain laurel

Oak- oleander-onion weed

Paddy melon-pasparphen ergot-Paterson's curse-perennial ryegrass at root level

Pheasant's rye, pokeweed-*privet

Quince

Ragwort-rattle pods-red maple-round Billy Button

Sagebrush-St. John's wort-sneeze wort -*salanaceae/in the deadly nightshade family

Potato

Stinging tree-stagger weed-Sudan grass

Thorn apple-tobacco plants-variegated thistle

*Water hemlock-white snake root-wisteria-Wooley head

Yellow star thistle-yew

Identification of all the above may take some discipline to learn. The best practice is to assume that anything other than your familiar grass or hay could be a possible killers. Go through your pastures and remove anything suspect. Do your research on these poisonous plants, especially those indigenous to your area, and see what they look like. It really is a wonder just how we've managed to keep our animals as safe as we have all this time. The misconception that animals will avoid what's harmful to them is simply not true. There are many more toxic plants that can't be added to this list, but I have generalized down to the most deadly I could find.

To suffer the loss of a beloved horse, who is often a member of the family, is something I don't ever want to go through. When a horse means so much to you, please take all possible precautions and be ever so diligent as to what goes into its stomach. To suffer the loss of a much-loved animal would be a lasting heartache...and never easily forgotten.

Lady Mo Pascoe-Hoyal

Chapter 18
Sir George

Looking across my friend's roping arena one cold January morning just two weeks after I'd given birth to my precious baby daughter, the weakness and pain that often accompanies delivery didn't deter me from admiring the horse flesh that was going 'round with their racing and roping lessons. It was 1967 and I was full into the Louisiana life, having come from Hawai'i...and boy did I experience an electrifying jolt of full-blown culture shock seeing what was still going on in 1964 when I first landed. Won't go there! But standing right before me that morning was a magnificent horse in all of his winter coat glory. He was tied to the outer railing of the arena fence, calm yet majestic, a beautiful black gelding with an arched neck and ears facing forward. He appeared to have the grace and beauty of a stallion. Something went off in the head and heart of this horsewoman. It was that special feeling which comes with inner certainty and an overwhelming magnetic pull toward that object of desire. I loved him from the first moment I laid my eyes upon him.

My initial ride gave me a good indication of how smooth and "in check" he was, unbelievably so, and how gentle a nature he possessed. I was very impressed and entranced. He stopped on a dime, turned rapidly with barely a touch, and I could use a "drop rein" on him from the "get-go." There went tax returns for that year. Wow! $400.00 for a million dollar horse! George was his name; he was middle-aged and not fast enough for the roping horse my "drug store cowboy" husband (at the time) thought he would be. After seeing him ridden and beaten with a hard riata to go faster-which didn't work I jumped in and told my husband the horse was not suitable for speed and that I wanted him.

We began training for Western Pleasure events. This gentleman of a horse also turned out to be nearly "bomb proof." Later on, and since my husband wouldn't watch my two babies, ages two and six months, for just one hour so I could ride and train, I then had to put baby girl in diapers in front and my young son behind me, holding on to Mommy. (Needless to say, I am no longer married to this man!) I literally put our lives into George's capable and gentle hooves and heart. When we went down the road to Aunty Skip's, who had a cutting horseman for a husband, these much-loved friends took my children and me under their wings. Skip being a "Ferner" from Ireland, she well understood the mindset I was dealing with in coming to the south. This dear friend watched my babies, who in turn became her babies from that day forward. I was so grateful to have this hour to train my horse. The results were amazing in that George only needed the love I gave to him. Training amounted to mainly just a tweak here and there. He did learn to immediately stop with just a softly spoken "hup" from me that the judges couldn't hear. He'd go from a standstill, right into a smooth-as-glass short lope with just a cluck of the tongue, also un- heard. I immediately "titled" him "Sir George" from that day forth. It was a name of honor that he greatly deserved. Proud was I, to hear his name announced over the loud speakers at every event we entered.

Many times did we ride down that little country lane; baby girl was rocked to sleep, and the only fear that presented itself was when I would sing the Ray Steven's song, "Talkin' Jones." Since we rode beside a railroad track, I'd say "Talkin' Jones" was coming out of the woods to tie us up on the railroad tracks. Instant tightening of little arms around my waist came from my son in the back of the saddle, which set me off to laughing so much! Hard as they were, I'll never forget those precious times. I got two birds with one stone. I was able to continue riding and bonding with babies and horses. Eventually, both kids turned out to be quite the little riders themselves on our faithful and steady Shetland pony, Dynamite. He was another rare find.

For a few good years, Sir George and I went 'round and 'round in those arena circles to any place we could haul. We won a lot of first-place trophies and many ribbons. This was the horse of my dreams. He was my personal "Black Beauty" from my childhood books, and I was very fortunate to have him. He was the steed of which little girls' dreams are made. The love we had for each other was clearly mutual.

After much consideration, I left Louisiana and went back home to Hawaii with my kids, leaving George with my husband. I had to see if we could save our marriage and that maybe after a brief separation, it would prove beneficial. When the lovely visit was over, it was time for us to return to Louisiana and work on our marriage. My husband had to sell my beloved George for the return airfare. It was a huge heartache for me, but I desperately wanted to keep my little family together. What really broke my heart further, though, was when my husband came home one day gloating over how my horse had stopped eating after he was sold and then died! There was no way for me to confirm any of this; I had no contact, and none was given. The worst part of this heartache was the fact that my husband could be so mean to me! This was the first time in all of my life that I had the full realization of what this kind of meanness was. I couldn't fathom that someone could do this to another human being. Buckets of tears ensued...buckets of them.

Life with my husband was never good after that. Even the house we bought with a big red barn and five good acres didn't feel the same. I did work hard to get our place in dandy shape, it was so pretty, and I loved the barn very much. I continued with horse ownership, but I stopped showing. George was one in a million, and his death took it all out of me. Having children, a two story house, then enough money and land, couldn't save our marriage, or even make it tolerable. One day I packed up my car, along with my babies and little Tater dog, and left for Nashville, Tennessee, to pursue my musical career.

All through the years, I never forgot my Sir George and how much beauty and love he brought to my life. I still cry at the very thought of how I was told of his passing and of how someone could be so mean-spirited to rub this kind of salt into existing wounds. To this day, I still have no proof that my George had died in the way it was described to me and by someone who was supposed to love me?

Presently, I have a gentle and loving black Tennessee Walking Horse mare, mother to eight or more, and protective of me as she was to her foals. But so far, no horse has come anywhere close to my beloved George; even as much as I do love this mare, I beg that Heaven exists and that he waits for me in some lush pasture. I've also asked for my Daddy to come riding up on him, to meet me when it's my time to go...and hoping of course, that Mama's waiting in Heaven's kitchen to sneak me in the back door!

Mosie Appleseed

Chapter 19
Ranger Little Love

When I brought that beautiful Palomino Welsh pony home three years ago, in order for my grandson to learn about horses, I hoped we'd eventually be able to ride together at some point. I didn't realize, however, that what I'd brought to my barn and to my loving mare was a regular tyrant! I felt Ranger was inappropriately named and should have been called Ivan The Terrible or Genghis Khan!

Most of us who have engaged with ponies know they tend to be bullied and can be quite ferocious at times. There is a definite reason for this, though. Ponies learn to intimidate at a very early age so their smaller selves don't get bullied and harmed by the larger horses in their herd. Ranger came from a ranch that stabled six or more very large horses. Living and interacting with him in just a short period of time, I could see he was terrified of large horses. So little Ranger, weighing in at about 500 pounds and was less than 14.2 hands in height, learned his lessons of intimidation very well. From a large ranch to my small place with only one gentle, welcoming mare didn't make things any better, nor was Ranger any less afraid. Not only did he bully "Lolly the Good", but he tried to bully Mo, the mother, grandmother of everybody, and very much the disciplinarian. "Oh no, little guy, that's not going to work here," I said to him one day after watching him try to pull his not-so-nice little pony stuff around our place.

Ranger, ah yes...his first tactic of intimidation with me was to bump right up and push on my midsection when he saw me coming with his feed tub. That only happened a few times before the orange training stick came with me. A loud, stern voice and a non-hurtful jab to his broad chest with the end of this stick of wonders had him backing up and waiting for his tub to be placed on the ground first. Ranger also learned he couldn't dig into it until I signaled with a pat to my knee that he could start eating. Aha, this can work, I thought. The next lesson came when I began grooming him, and he thought he would "cow-kick" me. A "cow kick" is slang used and understood by horses and cattlemen, and it's generally a striking out sideways of a rear leg, some of this done by cows during milking. However, it also applies to horses. Ranger tried this one day while I was grooming him. Tactic number two. I smacked his broad hind end sharply with the flat of my hand. It made a loud noise but it didn't hurt, and then I told him loudly, "Oh, no, you don't!" That got his attention, and he never did it again.

Next came the nip to my back when I was turned away from him. It was more like a pinch but still very painful. He did this in anticipation of a "cookie." I yelped loudly and quickly wheeled around so I could smack him, and he wheeled around and ran like the devil himself was after him. This told me he knew he'd done something wrong and that he possessed reasoning, another "Aha moment" for this not-so-little pony.

After all the hooliganism, even though he's Welsh, Ranger next worked on Lolly, who initially tried to be welcoming. He had no part of it and chased, bit, and kicked her, making her life a living nightmare. She had to be put into her stall at feeding times because Ranger would go for her portion after he gobbled up all of his. This bullying continued for quite some time until Lolly had taken enough of it. She caught Ranger in the shared, large stall one night after my chores had been done and I had gone in for the day. And imagine...she was still generous enough to share her stall with this little cuss during storms and cold weather. When I went out the following morning, I found that both sides of Ranger's upper rump were full of skinned patches, as in bald! Same for over his right eye. This was the ultimate lesson he learned from the mother of eight foals, and she was having no more of him! This action by Lolly took care of things around here from then on, and Ranger is now docile and obedient to her. This disciplinary action by a ticked-off mother mare also helped me. I guessed he thought he'd better stop going up against the two of us.

After our bad start, Ranger began to learn his manners for the barn, paddock, and humans. I planned a three-month beginner's horsemanship class for both my grandson and Ranger. How beautifully this turned out. It was like seeing magic unravel a beautiful thread of love and discipline right before my very eyes. I witnessed the development of a close bond between a nine-year-old boy and his pony of equal years. They took to each other, both learning, both loving. This course covered many areas...so unruly pony and young boy with focusing problems learned and surprisingly retained all they were taught. The key to respect was deeply ingrained in them. From the first time I put my grandson on Ranger, there was never another problem.

Now that Ranger's been with us these four years and has "grown up so nicely," I added "Little Love" to his name, giving him the entitlement that he is now a little Sir, a Little Lord, a Little Love. The only thing that persists is the pinning back of his ears, which he displayed ever since I got him. These little ears seem to have been permanently "sewn" back with an invisible thread of fear. Now, when I call him, and he comes, his head is bent in submission, but I know there's no malice behind the pinning back of his ears; he was just so afraid, and this, I feel, will be permanent damage to such a tender soul. In our own ways, we have achieved success because Ranger Little Love is no longer afraid.

With regard to the subject of bullying, I've seen it in the "pecking order" with my hens, and I've experienced it first-hand in the world of cows and horses many times over. However, my heart absolutely bleeds along with all of the parents who have lost their precious children to suicide caused by the bullying of their peers in school.

Bullying is something that should never be allowed in human society, and certainly not at my little barn.

I've been told all of my life, "You can't save the world, Mo," but oh, how I wish I could.

Lady Mo Pascoe-Hoyal

Chapter 20
Lolly, The Horse Who Saved Me

Being saved can have different meanings to us all. Here, in the deep southern bayou land, "Bible Belt" of Louisiana, "being saved" usually means you are a "born-again Christian," His follower, and devoted to the teachings of Christ. Therefore, you are saved by Jesus. You can also be saved from many other things, as when drowning, and you're plucked from perilous waters by a strong and saving hand, or from an automobile accident when you're pulled out of your burning car...so on and so forth. In my case, I was saved by a big black mare I renamed Lolly. I hang on to this mare's halter with a death grip because of the many times I fall down in trying to serve as an example of my faith, and quite often, I have despaired. For thirty years, I begged God to "Please let me have one more horse before I die!" This prayer was answered by the time I reached the age of 63, and while I'm now nearing 75, Lolly and I are still going strong. I have my very own "Black Beauty" of my childhood longing. The icing to this cake of longing would be for both of us to be in my beloved England.

Lolly came at a time when I thought my world was about to end. I am head-to-toe injured, but I thank God daily for the ability to still be able to walk. In addition to this, I've been married for 32 years to a non-recovering alcoholic. Troublesome doesn't even begin to describe him. So, my life had ebbed drastically, and if not for the love of my children, grandchildren, my sister and her family, I could have cared less if I lived or died. Quite frankly, death would have been a great relief because I am having a very hard time living with the kind of constant, burning pain that grips me 24/7. I have a fighting spirit and I'm always afraid I'll miss what's coming 'round the bend, and I figured I can't go before it's my time to be called... not the right thing to do. I'm not the only one in this world who carries a cross or has a too full plate. There's a lot to be gained from the adage, "Keep on keeping on." With all of this on me, I thought I must be stark, raving mad to let another horse come into my life, especially when the probable truth hit me between the eyes that this horse could very well outlive me!

When I first saw Lolly, I learned that her registered name was "Mystery Colors," a very beautiful name, but one that was never used in all of her thirteen years. She was a prospective purchase by me and when her owner, another friend, and I went to get her from the pasture, she took off running with her three daughters. I then went into the pasture with a halter held behind my back and just stood perfectly still. This wonder of mares walked right up to me. Her owner was amazed! Lolly let me put the halter on, and from that moment, it was sealed, and I knew she was to be mine. I got the same vibratory feeling from her as well. I rode her for two months before bringing her home and we got along very well, although she was too thin for my liking, and she had that dead "shark eye" look in her eyes. No sign of personality or "smarts" was displayed. Lolly also needed a lot of hoof care and more obedience training, mostly learning to be patient. It took over six months of love and good nutrition for her to start to come alive...and when she did, what a remarkable difference it made. With close to 100 pounds gained, Lolly became the sleek "Black Beauty" of my girlhood dreams. Her bloodlines run deep with a very good strain of Tennessee Walking Horse background and I couldn't be more proud to have her.

Mystery Colors is off the sire, Battle Colors, her dam, Mystery Caller. The name Lolly came by way of watching how she would lollygag around on trail rides when she wasn't being awful. Lolly doesn't like a confined ride (nose-to-tail), and neither do I. She has a fast walk and resented being behind a slower horse, so we ended our rides with those folks.

Along the Trail with Lolly

Since then, this mare has shown her love and protection for me for many years, and never has a former broodmare turned out to be such a nice ride under the saddle. Lolly is gentle, stops, and reins surprisingly well; spurs were never necessary. Just a cluck of the tongue from me, and she's ready to go. Lolly has even displayed very protective actions toward me, especially on three occasions. The first one happened when she saw me walking too close to a snake one day as I went to the mailbox. She frantically began snorting, pawing the ground, and running back and forth in the paddock in such a frenzy it caught my eye. "His eye is on the sparrow," and Lolly had her eye on me. I then saw the snake and backed away. Lolly didn't stop this behavior until I got to the safety of the front steps. The second time her display of protection came was when two nasty neighborhood dogs that were clearly displaying aggressive "pack mentality' entered her turf and headed for me. Those two canines didn't want a friendly pat on the head! Lolly bared her teeth, laid her ears back and dove into them. They ran for their lives, never to return. It must be the strong maternal instinct she has. The third time was very comical; two men who were in the paddock with me, quoting the cost for tree-felling soon got a scary surprise. As we stood debating over price, Lolly kept circling them, and very noticeably too. Of course, jester that I am, I played it up big and kept patting her, telling her it was all right. By the time those big men got ready to leave, I told them I'd open the gate for them. "No! No!" they hastily said, and both ran to the barbed wire fence, somehow getting through those five strands unscathed! Neither man got stuck while escaping, and their clothing remained intact. I got a laugh out of that one, and I'll never tell anyone again that Lolly is as "gentle as a lamb." She's my savior in these times. I believe that owning a beloved horse, along with laughter, can help to ease the many aches and pains that occur during the aging process...which is often very hard to accept.

The main thing Lolly has brought back into my life is a very strong feeling of love and bonding, a more positive attitude in feeling that yes, I still can. Prior to this, I was feeling my life was just about over and what on earth did I have to hang onto? Well, I don't easily discount my family, who love me, and also my four beloved grandchildren, who think I hung the moon and simply must live to be as old as Methuselah. I have a reason to rise every morning; hey, there are folks and critters out there who need me, and two of them are regular "hay burners!"

Riding now is no longer an option... and to think I once just grabbed a swatch of mane and jumped up with such ease to ride bareback all the live-long day. But if not for Lolly and the desire she has given me to be alive again, life is now worth more to me than all the gold on this planet. I hang tightly to her halter, and I pray an awful lot, so I can be a better person in this world, keeping to God's will and not to my own. And now... I'm begging God once more to "Please let me be with my horses in Heaven when it comes time for me to finally 'bite the dust of this earth. Amen!"

Mosie Appleseed

Photo Credit:

Mo Pascoe Hoyal, Pete Ferington, and Wayne E. Hoyal

Chapter 21
Sisters In Saddles

I always wanted to be with her. She had the air of freedom and rebellion. One afternoon, when her work day was over, Mo called and told our mother she was bringing a friend home to spend the night. Mom was okay with this news, got prepared to meet our visitor, and set an extra plate on the dinner table. When they arrived, we immediately saw who this guest was; a spirited, 4-legged, young grey roan horse named "Chiquita," who remained tied to a tree in the back yard overnight.

My big sister had such a powerful influence over me. I ran after her dressed in my cowboy shirts and boys' jeans and I was usually barefoot, except for when we were at the stables. Boots for that place!

Mo was a young horsewoman who surfed the beaches at Waikiki and was also a card-carrying member of The Screen Extras Guild. Remember "Ginger" from "Gilligan's Island?" Mo was "Ginger's" stand-in during the opening of the TV show. Yeah, that was her as Ginger boarding the "Minnow" every week! We were born in paradise...Honolulu, Hawai'i.

One day, Sis borrowed Dad's car, a '51 column shift Chevy with steel dashboard, seats covered in Scotch plaid, tire rims painted red, and NO SEAT BELTS BACK THEN! I was allowed to go with her!

On our way to Kapiolani Stables, built for our long-ago Queen Kapiolani, who loved horse racing, we'd get fries and soft drinks at the "Mynah Bird" drive-in. We hung out just being a big sis, treating her kid sis really well. When we got to the stables, Mo gave me a tour of the entire place and taught me how to brush one of the horses, instilling in me ground safety in the handling of this huge animal. She then fixed me up with "Comanche," an old "Paint," and told me I could ride all over the stables but not to leave the grounds. It was my first taste of freedom. Man, was I hooked!

When I got older, we "hot-walked" Polo ponies for the teams, some of which came from Argentina and Great Britain. Prince Phillip was a major attraction, and he was given use of the finest string of ponies our island club possessed. Hot-walking is cooling down an overly heated horse by slowly walking it around.

During extremely fast-paced matches, horses needed to be changed out for fresh ones. A game is divided into chukkers, typically four to six per game, usually lasting seven and one-half minutes, with four players on each team. We took pride in cooling off these horses. It was our job, and the exchange of horses had to be quick.

Mo and I took on this job very seriously, and with great pride. We were valued and treated with respect. Our Dad would drive us from one side of the island to the other so we could hot walk for the big matches held there. Dad was very outgoing and easily made friends at these events. He was proud of his girls being able to participate in a wonderful sport-"The Sport of Kings." And even though we were mainly in the background, we were on horseback! Without hot-walkers, there would be no Polo!

We were faced with snobbery at times, and we chose to hang out with the down-to-earth kids. One friend told us about a girl who was showing off by walking back and forth under her horse's neck until, annoyed, he bit her on her back. Well, sometimes Karma comes around.

Mo participated in Hunter Hack jumping events on a mount named "Cisco," who became nervous at one event and ran full speed over the jumps. Very dangerous! Mom covered her face and prayed her dare-devil daughter would remain safe in the saddle. Mo told me later she got dis- qualified for going at an unsafe speed.

I remember Dad taking Mom and I to our local King Kamemeha Day parade where Sis was riding with a group all dressed in traditional, sarong-like, satin material, (a Pa'u) which was wrapped around and fastened at the waist with a Hawai'ian kukui nut. It was the attire of the early horsewomen of our islands, when riding. It was all so cool.

Over the next few years, Mo gave me basic English riding lessons, which was not easy for me. All that posting...rising up and down in the saddle trying to match the inside lead of the horse as you go 'round in a riding ring. I was better at learning to sit a Western saddle.

By that time, Mo was settled in Louisiana with a family of her own and she participated in Western Pleasure events at local competitions. I left Hawai'i after we convinced our parents to let me go, and so I went to live with Mo and their family. Everyone needs to leave home for new adventures.

Sis got me my own horse the third day after I arrived. I mostly rode bareback, but when the heavy saddle was not in use by her husband, Mo taught me this new way of riding, and I was put through the paces, as well as my new "green broke" mare, who was still so young and needed a lot of training herself. Both horse and rider learned how to behave together.

On occasions when Mo participated in western events, her husband would hitch up the trailer, load her horse, and we'd all pile into his Dodge pick-up and drive to the afternoon or evening shows. I was so proud to be there. The $400.00 dollar horse Mo bought happened to be a great purchase in that he won many first-place trophies. Did I already mention how cool this all was?

In those early days while Mo's kids were in school, we'd saddle up and hit the back roads to our friends' ranch to exercise our horses, and

I'd put my steed through more obedience training. We also went riding through the rural neighborhood and sometimes had run-ins with horrible dogs owned by horrible people. Our horses always just put their heads down and kept walking without even so much as a kick towards a hound. That was usually the worst of it for me. I was never injured from a fall or by a rank animal. It was not the case for Mo, however.

Over several years, Mo suffered many injuries and is now paying for several more that followed, and is very limited in what she can physically do. She has traded her outdoor gardens for hydroponic units and now grows indoor gardens. Mo has also had to give up sewing for her grandchildren, which makes her sad. We correspond by e-mail these days and talk on the phone, reminiscing about our youth. We laugh a lot over the funny times, and there were many!

Though we live in different states, it doesn't affect the spiritual closeness we have and always will have. Some things don't change, and even though our bodies have aged, we still feel like the kids we were in our hearts.

Bless you, dear Mo, sister of mine. I will always remember the kindness in your being and the free spirit your soul possesses. I love you to the moon!

Paula Abbott

Chapter 22
The Bar B Que Derby

As I looked up, I realized I was lying on the ground between two legs and hooves. I saw her belly with the girth strap still firmly in place. Next, I saw a man's arm reach out and take hold of the reins, all the while speaking to her in soothing tones. This man, my Guardian Angel or perhaps The Good Samaritan, knew horses. I also noticed the sleeve of the Aloha shirt he was wearing. He called out to nearby people to "Get an ambulance!" It's a good thing I blacked out just after this because I didn't feel her hooves stepping all over the bottom half of my body, starting from my hips to my feet. Our family doctor originally thought my right hip was broken. My right thigh muscle had been severed and turned as black as the horse I was riding. I was on crutches for two or three months. This is the beginning of my story that most likely could have been the end of me, and it was the day I rode home with a man I didn't recognize. I know it broke his heart when I kept asking him along the ride home, was he really my Daddy?

It was my ride of rides that took place on a beautiful Saturday afternoon, in the perfection of the Hawaiian Islands that was home to me those many years ago. I was about 16 and had charge of my best friend's horse, Diablo, for the entire weekend. I never made it to Sunday!

During Saturday's ride, we were gently cantering on the trail that circled the Polo enclosure with accompanying bleachers along the exterior path of the Polo field. The Kapiolan'i Park's picnic area to the right of me was just next to this Polo field's trail. For some reason unknown to me until after the accident, Diablo bolted and began to run at full gallop as she headed right for the people who were trying to enjoy their hibachi lunches. I was screaming for them to get out of the way. I couldn't stop her, and turning her into circles would have been too dangerous for the speed she was going. I saw the looks of pure horror on people's faces who were grabbing their children, hurrying to get out of our way. I screamed all along the park for people to "Get out of the way!" I had absolutely no control, and Diablo may have taken the bit into her mouth as well. We didn't stop until we reached the far end of the stables itself, as she came to an abrupt halt when we reached the 8' fence she couldn't jump. This is when I hit the ground.

Diablo was a high-strung, beautiful black mare who was kept feisty by her owner, Denise, the hell-bent for leather, dare-devil rider. Denise was a fantastic rider who could ride anything, but she was a rider who also kept all of her horses "hopped up." Denise always went like her own tail was on fire and she brought this feeling to her horses, who picked up on this kind of thing. A horse's 6th sense knows when we are nervous, frightened, or generally upset, and it transfers to them immediately. I was a good rider and kept my seat the whole time, however, only until we reached that fence. Diablo had remained calm when we first started out and I had wondered if she got spooked by something of which I wasn't aware. I HAD NO CONTROL! I later found out the leather curb strap broke and there we have it.

My next remembrance was being brought home by this man I didn't know. I was on crutches, my thigh muscle was severed, my right shoulder and chin had skinned patches on them, and my left ankle was shaved to the bone. Don't ask me how that happened, I was wearing boots. Recovery was slow and painful, and I missed school time also. Concussed, I spent two days in amnesia, which ensued after the accident, and later, I went to a friend's class to relate this incident to them while they were on the subject of amnesia. I was only aware of being in a car and looking to my left and seeing this man I didn't know. All of the color had been removed from my world. What was a usual full technicolor day in beautiful Hawai'i turned into a black-and-white world. This surrounded me all the way home. Riding was out for months, which killed my soul, but I healed and did live to get back up in the saddle again. If you do not get back up in the saddle, you may as well quit for the rest of your life. You have to overcome the fear. It took me quite some time to get my nerves again, and I was alright for years until I became quite a lot older. When in my 60's, the fear came back, and it caused my own gentle black mare to become nervous. Here again was the transference from rider to mount and proved so true by me.

I'm now a retired, disabled, former equestrian with a lot of miles behind me, on top of me, under me, and all around me. I've sustained much damage, the worst being the spine injuries and nerve damage. The pain from this nerve damage is unbearable. I pray for the mercy which will only come with death. I do good to still hobble around with a walking stick. I refuse to give in to the wheelchair, but I know one day soon, that wheelchair will be more than just a looming picture at the back of my mind. I mostly stay at home. My bed and television are my best friends. Due to a tailbone fracture long ago, sitting has become a horror, and for one who loves to write, sitting becomes your worst enemy. Still, I hold to the sanctity of life, choosing to suffer with a loving family around me rather than doing the abominable easy way out. I will gladly accept a prayer from anyone who happens to read my story. There are a lot of us in this world who suffer, and I am not trying to act as though I am the only one. I still prepare the evening meals, and I continually utter to God to help me. I also say the Hawaiian word, "Imua," which means to go forward, this I will adhere to until God decides when my time is up!

By: Lady Mo Pascoe-Hoyal (Fiasco Pascoe of old)

Chapter 23
Horse Whisperer

My daughter calls me a "horse whisperer." Far from it, I say. The truth about "horse whispering" holds to a common factor I discovered while reading all of the pages of research I avidly pored over in order to write this article. That common factor is the use of empathy in the ways of training a horse. Love, kindness, gentility, and never brutality, or the breaking of the horse's spirit as was done in the days of the old west when horses were needed in a hurry and were hastily trained in what we now consider to be a very crude and harsh manner. You get a much better animal when you use the calmer and more gentle way of training, and you also get a horse that learns to trust you, which is the most important characteristic of all. My baby daughter started out riding with me and her older brother at the tender age of 6 months while she was still in diapers. My then-husband would not care for them for the one hour I needed to continue training my show horse, so I had him hand her to me to put in front while two-and-a-half-year-old big brother rode behind me. Four little arms held dearly to me. We had a splendid horse who was so calm and gentle that he could be trusted with my babies on board. He was just plain old George when I bought him. After learning his noble and gentle ways, I "titled" him "Sir George." He won every first-place trophy in all of the Western Pleasure classes I entered, except for one when he became nervous for some unknown reason by me. However, he took second place instead. I was proud to hear my name announced and prouder still to hear, "on Sir George" as we entered the show ring. I could use a drop rein on him and utter "Hup" under my breath without opening my mouth, and he would come to a complete stop without me having to pull on the reins. He was the most impressive horse I have ever owned, and jet black, my favorite color for a horse.

Going as far back as the Native Americans and their ways of training, they'd first ride one of their own horses within a wild herd and latch onto a particular horse they wanted. Once this wild horse knew it wasn't getting away and was usually tired down, the gentle methods of the Native Americans were then applied, and these horses became devoted and obedient animals. They learned to stay put when their reins were dropped to the ground, never leaving that spot. The horse was an integral part of the Indian Nations, and horses served many purposes. Some carried warriors to battle, others carried women and children. Many horses were trained to pull a travois, a French Canadian word for what is also called a drag sled. The use of the travois enabled the nomadic tribes to move tepees and other items along their many journeys. Some were used to carry children and maybe the elderly or the sick and infirm. The Native Americans were all fascinating people who made everything they needed from earthly content. I would say they were the first "horse whisperers."

When the white Europeans first came to the shores of the east coast of the Americas, they took over parcels of land that the Native Americans used to care for. The Native Americans never considered owning the land, but rather, they were the caretakers. Wars ensued over land, and many Native Americans were killed. Those who remained were herded off to reservations on the poorest of lands. It was one of the cruelest moves anyone could make upon another human being and to have them forcefully removed from the areas they considered to be their homes. If you know about "The Trail of Tears," you will understand what I am speaking about. Many other cultures have been enslaved, but here we are speaking of our Native Americans.

The Army needed mounts, so here is where most of the cowboys entered the picture. They captured horses from wild herds and broke them in for fast use, while most of the time, they broke the horse's spirit along with it. These cowboy methods of training were often brutal and harsh, bending the will of horse to man. This way of training horses lasted for decades until other people entered the picture with their new and gentle ways of training.

In come the "Horse Whisperers." Many believe there is a certain magic that a horse whisperer has, and with some, it is like a form of magic, yet were you to ask one who is termed a horse whisperer, they'd quickly deny that. The magic is in the kind ways a horse is trained. The word empathy factors in a big way here. If you remember the old English adage, "You catch more flies with honey than vinegar," you will quickly get the idea of how gentle training will bring the horse running up to you. Bad training has some owners running after their horses with halters behind their backs before the horse lets itself be caught and then stands still for the halter to be put on. I wouldn't have a horse who'd run from me. All of the horses I've ever trained always came running up to me. I use what I call "The Cookie Method." Like most humans and animals alike, horses can be ruled by their stomachs. When great food is served, people flock to restaurants. It works on husbands too! Whenever I got a new horse, I would immediately identify myself to this horse with a carrot, an apple piece, or even a horse treat found at most farm and feed stores. Once I got my new horse hooked on my cookie method, that horse would forever run up to me when called, and I never chased one down again! My last two here would come up to me whether I had a cookie or not, and they both followed me around the paddock if I stopped to talk to a neighbor by the fence. They'd stand on either side of me or behind me the whole time. This last mare I had also walked in circles around two men who entered the paddock one day to give me a quote for cutting down a dead tree. They left scrambling for the barbed wire fence even after I offered to open the gate for them. Her strategic manner of encircling them as we spoke was enough for them to be totally spooked by such a gentle mare. She was in her protect Mama mode. I never let on to these guys that she was gentle because she didn't express that with her body language. I have to admit I got a laugh from what happened on this particular day. Two grown men running for barbed wire instead of simply letting me open the gate.

Basically, people who we call "Horse Whispers" are a bit more than ordinary people, they genuinely love the horse and make the ways of the horse their life study. They can see that the putting back of ears and the baring of teeth mean anger! They look for moods: depression, ill health, teeth, hooves, conformation, abuse, poor nutrition, fear, anger, loneliness, happiness and well-being etc.; some breeds of horses are calmer, like the draft horses, while others are feisty like the Arabians. These are only two of the many breeds of horses the world over. Observation is the mutual aspect of horse management and training among all of these horse handlers. They study and learn the ways of the horse. Gentle and calming tones are used over harsh words of anger. Anger and harsh handling will never get you anywhere, and you can end up with a vile horse. If you ask any or all of whom are considered to be "Horse Whisperers," they all have the "Magical" ways of kindness, gentle handling, soft tones and understanding in common.

Here are a few people who are called "Horse Whisperers": Monty Roberts, Pat Parelli, Buck Brannaman, Carl Hester and Stacy Westfall. You can find them online and read about the ways they train horses. All of them train with kindness and gentility. Monty Roberts is often considered to be the "original horse whisperer." He's known for his method of what is called natural horsemanship, along with the concept he calls "Join Up" for his communication with horses. Monty knows and has studied the horse very well for decades.

Pat Parelli is also a known person in the field of natural horsemanship, and he has developed a training program based on horse psychology.

Buck Brannaman is a very respected horse trainer who has been influential in the development of humane training methods.

Carl Hester is a British dressage rider and trainer. He has made significant contributions to the understanding of horse behavior and training.

Stacy Westfall is recognized for her bareback and bridle-less riding techniques, and she also communicates with horses by using body language.

All of these people have made a name for themselves by promoting a deeper understanding and a more empathetic way of horse training. If horse owners, riders, and trainers would opt for the gentle way of handling the horse, we'd have less accidents, finer horses and better people!

Books by:

Monty Roberts- "The Man Who Listens To Horses," "The Story of a Real-Life Horse Whisperer" Pat Parelli- "Natural Horse-Man Ship," "Six Keys to a Natural Horse-Human Relationship" Buck Brannaman- "Faraway Horses," "Groundwork: The First Impression"

Carl Hester- "Making It Happen," "Down To Earth Dressage: How To Train Your Horse and Enjoy It"

Stacy Westfall- "Smart-Start: Building a Strong Foundation for Your Horse," "Basic Groundwork" with Stacy Westfall-2 DVD collection

*All of these books and more by the above trainers can be found at: www.amazon.com or any major book sellers online.

By: Lady Mo Pascoe-Hoyal

Research: Bing

Reading from Monty Roberts, and television shows about him.

Chapter 24
A Good Horse Can Harm You

Speaking from years of experience, yes, a good horse can harm you! Most of it will come from human error, a new-to-you horse who hasn't yet developed trust in you, or one that has not been trained properly by someone else when you purchased it. Case in point...my wanna-be cowboy neighbor came galloping down our blacktop road one day while I was out front doing yard work. I noticed his horse was thin and gimpy on his front hooves. I yelled at him to stop, then proceeded to take my smaller self with hands on hips and told him he was riding a lame horse on a hard surface at a gallop. Instead of a walloping that he could have easily given me, he turned out to be a rather nice guy who must have learned motherly obedience early on, even though we were the same age.

This horse was a lovely gelding, red-bay with black mane and tail. I offered him $100.00 on the spot. He gave his horse over right away and I immediately took this animal to the barn and gave him some water and a bit of grain after he was well cooled off. He needed a lot of work...he needed me! "Rebel" turned out to be a gentle and loving horse who was also very obedient. Dear Red Kelly, (RIP) an award-winning Farrier in our Tri-State area, just happened to be a good friend of many years and was a friend to most of my horses as well. Red came right over after I told him about this horse's condition. It took a full six months of special trims, care, and shoes to get Rebel back to where he needed to be. Rebel also filled out and was so beautiful, but, and I have to say, here comes the true colors of this horse... since we didn't know each other very well, his trust factor in me was a bit slow in coming.

He'd be perfectly fine around the neighborhood. He was good with my children. All was good until I had to cross cattle gap one day to lengthen our ride. There was a fence nearby with a latch on one post that opened to let riders get around the cattle gap. Entering another world went just fine. The mud puddle we walked through going out was still there on the way back but Rebel must have found a way around it the first time. When I reopened that wire gate on the way home, Rebel was afraid of going through the puddle since horses are said to be unable to judge the depth of water. Since he hadn't enough trust built up in me yet, he reared up and put me between his chest and front legs. I was pushed face-down into the puddle, and Rebel stepped on my back as he went through, using me as a bridge to get to the other side. I did notice that as soon as he felt he was stepping on me, he then lifted his hoof, but by then, it was too late; the damage had already been done. It was clearly my fault in assuming Rebel would just continue as he'd done when we first went out the wire gate. Nope! Not this time! I guess he was a rebel that day.

Many years later, as that area between my shoulder blades had become a problem with pain, I had a scan done that diagnosed scoliosis. This is where Rebel stepped hard enough on my back to push 5" of vertebrae off to the right. It is very painful now, especially with arthritis setting in. It hurts when coughing, speaking, and sometimes when merely inhaling and exhaling. I've stopped making phone calls because of this, combined with a neck injury sustained from an auto mishap later on. If Rebel had stepped on my back as hard as he could have, he very well may have broken it, and my family would have found me drowned and deceased in that mud puddle when they went looking for me. Rebel...he trotted back home to the barn. Fortunately, I was able to get up and walk the short distance home while covered in mud. Mama saw a horse come in with an empty saddle; she began to worry until she saw me trailing along behind, covered in mud. Then she laughed...not knowing the peril this accident brought to me all these many years later. This accident was clearly the result of human error. I should have let the horse go ahead of me, then turned him around so I could close the gate instead of trusting him too soon. I've seen and I've been through too many human error accidents all throughout my years of riding and training. The majority of these accidents were my fault!

I now feel I could give safety classes to adults and children, and never letting them mount a horse on their first lesson. Newbies to riding and the horse, most of all, must learn groundwork, learn about the horse and its possible foibles, and the many behavioral signs to look for. During my first riding lesson when I was twelve, I was just hoisted up on an English saddle before I could even learn to sit with hands and feet in proper positions and first to walk around. I was asked to canter, not knowing how to use my legs for support. I skidded along the ground on my belly for what seemed an age before I stopped and was made to get up in the saddle again, which was the right thing for me to do, but wrong, wrong, wrong for making a green student canter on their first lesson. The worst thing about my first lesson was that it was given to me by a very rough Polo player who just wanted to get it over with since it wasn't part of his egotistical forte! Later on, however, this man and I became friends. He liked my Dad a lot and they enjoyed visits whenever it was time for me to be picked up from the stables. So, that portion of my life ended well.

In all of the years that ensued, I sustained too many injuries because I adopted a "hell-bent for leather" approach to riding. I did things I shouldn't have, and rode fractious horses I had no business riding. I'm paying for all of the recklessness now and was deemed totally disabled at age fifty, yet I continued to ride a beloved mare of mine until I reached age sixty-nine. I had planned on riding a lot longer until pain completely took over one day, making it impossible for me to even gently walk her around. Giving up this mare and her stable pony buddy broke my heart. The barn, paddock, and pasture are empty. No animals remain to run and graze on the open land they left behind one very sad day in May four years ago. I won't even begin to tell you about all of my injuries, but they can be conducive to ones received by bronco busters or old cowboys from days gone by. I do good to hobble about now. I still want to grab a swatch of mane and hoist myself up and ride bareback as I once did. That dream will never go away. To be able to run with the breeze through my hair, bareback and barefoot, is freedom! It's only a memory now and I suppose I'm "lucky" to still be alive, so I've changed direction and just write about it these days.

To the wanna-be riders out there, don't end up like me. Take this as a lesson from a once formerly "oft air-headed" girl and learn how to handle and ride horses properly. Many of you will not want to listen, and if not, that's on you, but I pray having all of this experience behind me, that you really need to listen to people who are older and wiser than you. My medical charts read, "Head-to-toe permanently injured." You do not want this to be your diagnosis, please!

***And Rebel should never have been named as such because there wasn't one rebellious bone in his whole body except for that one day. I should have changed his name and he'd have gotten used to it like some of my others did when I didn't like the names they were originally given.

Lady Mo Pascoe-Hoyal

Chapter 25

Horse Ownership... The Strong Desire

Torture! It can be the worst feeling in the world to want a horse, especially when you can't get one. You either don't have the money, your parents don't have the land, and you are too young to impress upon your parents that you simply must have a horse! Tantrums didn't work in our family and I wasn't prone to them because I was a shy and sensitive child, very thoughtful and observant even at an early age. I'd pet everything on four hooves-if it would let me. When I became old enough to have a bit of a voice, like at age 8 or so, I had a sweet 16-year-old friend who'd let me sit on her horse as he grazed in an empty lot while she visited with neighborhood friends. That was a really big deal but in time it wasn't enough for me. I'd want Kane' (Hawaiian pronunciation Kah-nee) to move more than a few inches at a time and since I didn't know how to ride, Gail couldn't allow me to use her gentle, fat, black gelding just to walk up and down the little country road even though it had very little traffic.

I'd watch every television movie about horses, every series: "My Friend Flicka," "The Lone Ranger" with his magnificent horse, Silver, and anything that had horses in it. "Mr. Ed" and "The Black Stallion" came along many years later. I voraciously read every horse book that came out and I well remember crying at breakfast one morning and telling my mother I was very upset because she didn't name me Sybil. That one threw her for a loop, and I wouldn't tell her that I just finished reading a horse story where Sybil was a girl who owned a horse. Sybil?

Why in heck would I want to be called Sybil? In reality, I also hated my given name, which was Mary Elizabeth, and changed that over time!

My soul was awakened and revived when we moved into town, and I was enrolled in a Parochial school. When I attended Sacred Hearts Academy, I met the very horse-crazy Bonnie, who proved to be my very best horsey friend. Bonnie turned me on to the Kapio'lani Stables, where we rode to our heart's content. It wasn't easy for me at first, though. We had to pay to ride.

We lived in a 10-unit apartment complex, and every Saturday would find me, at age 12, washing and waxing every car that parked there. The tenants knew an idiot when they saw one because I washed their cars for a dollar and washed and waxed them for probably two dollars or so. I did a good job and had regular customers every week. Oh, why the heck not! I could ride all day on Sunday. The cost for horse rental back then was $4.00 an hour. I was very enterprising, and my parents were proud of me because I found a way to earn money at an early age in order to do something for myself.

Meanwhile, I took lessons that led me to caring for other people's horses so I could ride for free. After I became a good enough rider, I was hired by Mr. Dailey, who owned a string of polo ponies. Now, I could ride any of the five horses in my charge. Gaslight was my favorite, a big black Thoroughbred- mix and Mr. Dailey let me use him for local horse shows. Mr. Dailey also paid me a whopping $100.00 a month, which was good money back then. Wow! By the age of 15, I'd really climbed the ladder to the top of the horse! I loved horses so much, and I also enjoyed the work, manual labor being my favorite. I was able to buy my own first horse at age 16 when I could work at the local pineapple cannery.

I had many good years with horses but I also sustained a lot of accidents. In spite of it, I prayed for just one more horse before I died. That prayer lasted thirty years because life got in the way. I was injured in an auto crash on top of it all and moved to other locations. When I finally settled back in Louisiana with a Work Comp settlement large enough to buy a plot of land and the first mobile home, it was then the horse came back into my life again... prayer answered! I was still able to do some work, so beyond what the settlement paid for, I earned enough to put up a small barn and feed room and paid for all of the fencing and gates. I then earned enough to get my eighth horse, which turned out to be a she- devil and I quickly sold her to a friend. Then came "Lolly, the Great!" She was a "10" like a Bo Derek kind of horse to me, all black and feisty and of exceptional breeding. She was my first Tennessee Walker gaited horse and the side-to-side motion was much better than bouncing up and down.

Lolly and I spent thirteen wonderful years together, and I even got a pony to be her stall mate, but his behavior was so bad at first that she hated him! Ranger tried to rule, and you don't rule a mama horse who had 8 foals under her belt! So, Ranger learned his lesson one night when Lolly kicked the living daylights out of him as she caught him in the stall where he couldn't get out. He looked like he'd been through a battle the next morning. I never heard the commotion. Since that night little Welsh stallion-acting pony held his head bent in her presence as if saying, "Yes, Ma'am!" from then on.

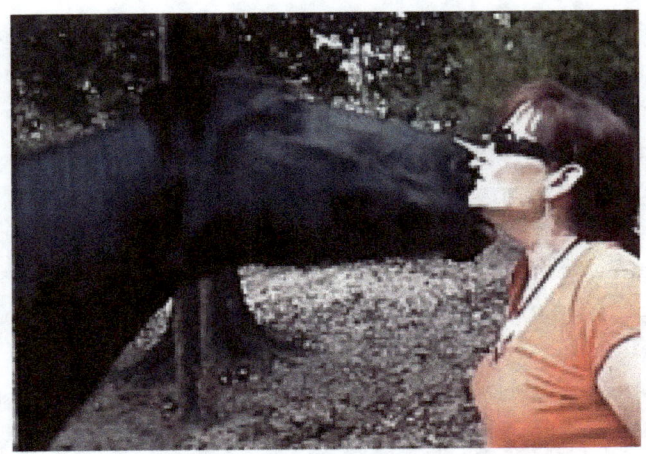

When spinal injuries became too painful for me to care for them and to ride, I sadly had to give both of my babies away. Anyone who tells you they are just animals, can go to blazes in my heart and soul. They did go to a beautiful ranch with lush green grass and are being well cared for. The heart still aches in spite of it. These are the very last animal heartaches I will ever endure for the rest of my life! Well...I still have two loving cats who remain my bedside companions.

The horse is a sentient being, meaning it can process emotion, it can have cognitive abilities, display loss and does mourn. The horse can also show depression or exhilaration, much love and gentility. It is born of pure innocence and made to be good or bad by whomever handles it.

I can't remember what first drew me to the horse, perhaps it's beauty, as I was only about three years old when I became overwhelmed at the sight of one. My love for the horse never went away and is still with me even now into my age as an old crone. I'll die wanting to ride in that "Happy Place." I pray daily to be able to go to a "Happy Place," a place where I can be with horses. I've loved my former dogs too. Maybe Leonard, my white lab rat, will be there to still ride on my shoulder like he did at school every day. I especially want to be able to be with wee children who went before their time and to teach them how to ride, grow vegetables, sing, and to draw pictures. I want us to be able to have pony carts full of fruit and vegetables to bring to all of our elders or anyone else who resides there. I want to be extremely busy and to work extremely hard, to be void of all of this bodily pain and old age that I hate with a passion. I guess by now you have probably well assumed that I live in a dream world. It's my world, however, and I want it just the way I see it. I believe I've earned it by trying hard to be as good as I could possibly have been. I suppose I'll find out at some point, but for now, I can only remain the dreamer I was born to be and I can only now write about it. And... just like music, art, or any of the fine talents we are born with, this innate feeling never goes away. Sometimes, it's hushed and locked away in one of the many compartments we all have within us. Often, we go back in time and become sad. We even cry as I still do with the overwhelming feeling every morning that I need to hurry through and not want to sleep in because there are beautiful and docile creatures outside who love me and who are hungry.

To hear the whinnies and nickers they expressed as soon as they saw me coming out the back door is forevermore a thing of the past. These days, I regale in that past and the feast that was set before me, all those many years ago. The "feast" of beauty, love, friendship, and the ability to be able to ride an animal and to have gentle command over it in all of its strength. For this great creature to come to me of its own free will and for us to be as one, melded together into the same sentient being, is the greatest feeling of pure magic I will ever know and experience!

Lady Mo Pascoe-Hoyal

Photo Credit:

Wayne E. Hoyal

Chapter 26
Never Give Up

In "Never Give Up," Season 6, Episode 7, of Chris Cox's Horsemanship show, I watched with anguish, familiarity, and compassion to what happened to J.R. Vezain, now a paraplegic rider who was disabled by a horse going over backward with him. He was entered in a rodeo bareback bronc event. Not only did the bronc go over backward, but it also slammed him up against the ground, folding his Thoracic spine in half at number T-10, causing serious injury to J.R. and rendering him numb and paraplegic from the waist down for the rest of his life. I could very well sympathize with J.R. because this very same thing happened to me one day when training a green broke filly. I was the fortunate one here as I landed in a recently dug furrow, and the saddle horn missed my belly by a mere few inches as it slid to the right side of me. I somehow scrambled off before the mare could get back up and later called her owner to come get her. Once this kind of thing happens to me, that's it. Call it "chicken" or whatever you like; I won't be mounting anything that does that kind of thing, feeling it may very well happen again once she got the hang of it by getting rid of her rider. I gave up that day! God spared me and I was just sore. I went home to lie down and rest. I also had two wee children and horses of my own waiting there and I was blessed because paralysis didn't take my legs from me, especially when I had so much to do and so many responsibilities in my young life. I am thankful! I do relate to J.R's aftermath of scans, therapies, surgeries, and a long recuperation/recovery period. Oh dear God, the frustration this young man must have endured, besides the trauma that changed his life forever!

J.R. was husband, father, and fellow horse lover... but he never gave up! Also to be considered was the potential huge medical costs just for him to get into the wheelchair.

Chris' show featuring J.R. Vezain it showed him back up in the saddle, with Chris having him to go through the paces of lead changes and all that encompasses working with your horse. J.R. uses straps around his thighs, fixed to the saddle, to help him with balance, and if you look very closely, his feet just wiggle around a bit in the stirrups. Chris teaches many facets of training and features riders like J.R. and others. This particular showcasing was especially inspiring since this same kind of accident happened to me, and I escaped possible paralysis or death myself. Chris is a wonderful human being. He is a humanitarian, rancher, family man, teacher, and more, and he also believes in Jesus Christ as his Savior. I feel this belief alone has made this great cowboy, Chris Cox, into who he is and what he stands for! And... what cowgirl wouldn't love to have her own personal Chris Cox?

J.R. had many fears and doubts since he was also a family man. The accident happened to J.R. in 2018, and by 2024, we see him up in the saddle again and fearless. A feeling of pride mixed with goosebumps swelled up in my entire being as I watched him ride. You go, guy! What good man wouldn't absolutely go to hell and back with all that fear of the future hitting him daily as he lay in a hospital bed, going home to another bed and then only to a wheelchair for his new way of traveling? J.R. got back in the saddle and lives to ride again, this time in the arena at the beautiful Triangle C Ranch in the wonderland of Wyoming. This article is basically about J.R. Vezain and his attitude of never giving up, but it also features Chris Cox, who holds clinic classes for adults and children alike, teaching them the safe way to handle horses and to ride. Chris is also a 4-time winner of "The Road To The Horse" and was inducted into the Cowboy Hall Of Fame in

2015. I admire both of these men! The Chris Cox Horsemanship program can be found on RFD TV.

In the world of horses, especially when entering events in rodeos, the rides can be dangerous, not only in the events of bucking horses but also in others like roping, steer wrestling, barrel racing, jumping in English riding events, and any other classes or events that usually involve speed, sound judgment or endurance while competing and staying on your mount. Anyone wanting to be in this world of horses should be properly trained and also given insight into the possibilities of accidents that can be expected to happen. I sincerely doubt on the day of J.R. Vezain's rodeo competition that, he negatively thought he may be critically injured or even killed. This is the chance we take, and no one is exempt from the many accidents that happen in this world. I wish J.R. the best of everything. He has proved endurance, "if at first you don't succeed, try again," and just gut-bustin' manhood, to have gone through all he had to go through in order to get from wheelchair- to back in the saddle again. I thank Chris Cox for showcasing J.R.Vezain on his program, and I highly encourage all who can to watch this very informative television show that comes to you readily available on RFD TV. God Bless you two men, you are both truly special and much-loved cowboys! Remember that patience, encouragement, and "individualized approaches are essential when working with disabled riders."

At the beginning of J.R.Vezain's recuperation, a whole other story can be found online under the title of "Despite a broken back, J.R. Vezain was unwilling to put his passions aside," or just search for a Bio about him. He first received a phone call from Aaron Brookshire, which was the moment that changed J.R.'s life! Also joining with brothers Marcus and Morgan Luttrell on their podcast in 2020, they spotlight "individuals who have been forced to persevere through challenges to survive." This podcast was instrumental in furthering J.

R.'s quest to getting back in the saddle again. The brothers sat down with Vezain to discuss his life after his accident. Vezain also happened to be a 6-time Wrangler National Finals Rodeo qualifier. This podcast led to a trail of physical therapy and to Vezain's strong will to chase for gold. His life is different now, and it wasn't how he had ever imagined it to be. However, he still chases his dream nonetheless. His quote: "Whatever successes the Lord brings me, I'm OK with. That's fine. But I can't NOT shoot for the stars." He just keeps going like the "Energizer Bunny"... only with cowboy boots'

*Like me, I don't know why J.R. didn't jump off before his horse went over on top of him. Maybe his hand was stuck in the rope. I had a man on the ground holding this mare, and even he couldn't prevent her from going over backwards... but we rode 'em to the ground, didn't we?

Lady Mo Pascoe-Hoyal

Chapter 27
To Shoe Or Not To Shoe?
(That Is The Question)

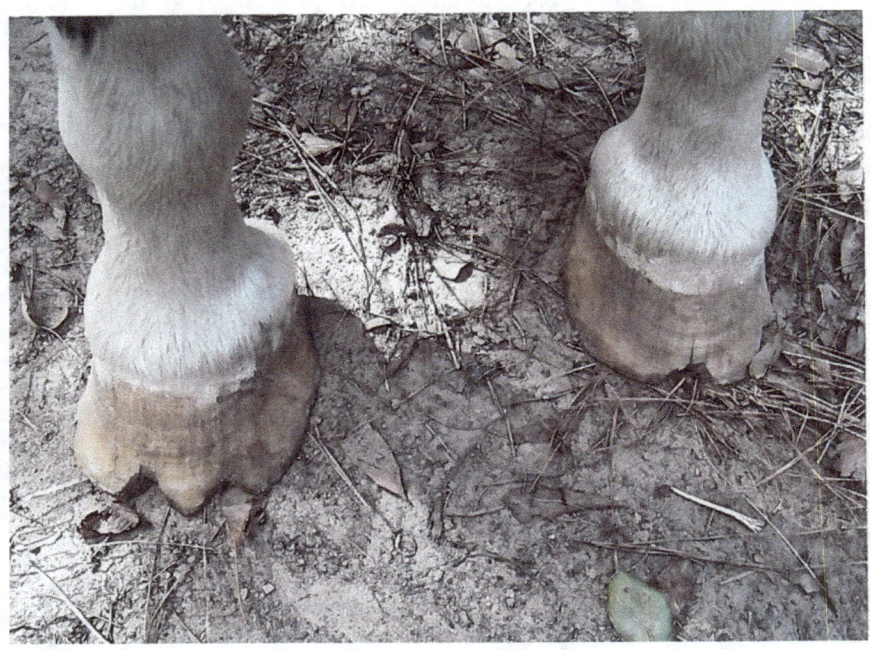

In my experience, and I can only speak for me and what I've gone through in horse ownership, shoeing depends on what kind of hooves your horse happens to have. The best hoof I've ever seen and had anything to do with came on my rather large Welsh pony, who had black hooves. They were absolutely brilliant for strength and resilience. They never chipped, cracked, he never went lame and I didn't feel the need to put shoes on him. My mare, on the other hand, came to me with bad hoof rot from being kept in a boggy pasture. My Vet carved large v-shaped chunks out of all four hooves, and this looked horrid until I could get my farrier, par excellence, to finish the task of hoof healing with proper trims and good shoeing practices. She was the worst horse I've ever had for bad hooves yet she never went lame through all of her treatments. I made sure this mare stayed shod, and I was vigilant about when to have shoes changed. Most of my horses were shod; as was the practice on the island I came from, because most were used for events such as roping, jumping, barrel racing, Polo, herding cattle on large acres of inferior land, and a lot of them were working horses. The only ones back home left unshod were the stable's rental horses who were ridden in safe areas or in riding rings for lessons. However, all of them had proper trimming and were well cared for. At one point in time, I fought hard against the new theory that all horses didn't need shoes, "The barefoot way," that was all the rage! A group of people I once rode with expressed to me that horses didn't need shoes, which was pure B.S. in my opinion, especially in my horse's case, and because of all the hell, care, and worry I had to go through to get her sound again. Their mindset proved to me that I was riding with a large number of ignoramuses who generalized all horses into the same category, and this also showed me a contagious view of ignorance this bunch of "experienced" and haughty horse owners had. I am not a follower nor easily led by a ring through my nose. I wouldn't cave to their pressure because I KNEW MY HORSE! I also felt that shoes kept the hoof safer, especially when riding the unknown trails, we traversed.

There are many pros and cons to shoeing a horse or keeping it barefoot, it really depends on the horse. A good suggestion is to get with your Veterinarian and a reputable Farrier first of all, unless you think you know enough about your horse to make your own decision. Shoes depend on conformation, condition, and type of hooves, ankles, legs, and how the horse moves when barefoot. Shoes can help in many conditions, and I am one who happens to believe in shoeing a horse, especially when the horse is used in hard work, ridden on rough terrain, and when corrective measures are necessary. Some barefoot horses can acquire cracks that are very difficult to maintain and put a stop to even with regular trimming and filing. If I had a horse with good hooves and it spent most of its time in pasture or as a companion to small children and only ridden around the homestead, I'd leave that horse unshod. However, if my horse was going to be used for barrel racing, trail riding, and more rigorous riding, I'd be quick to have shoes put on this animal. Some form of shoes has been used since 400 BC, first by using plants some kinds of materials, and usually wrapped around the entire hoof instead of being made of metal and nailed on. Even way back then, humans found a need for hoof protection.

If you're unsure about what to do or if you're a novice horse owner, the best advice I can give you is to consult with a professional. There is a reason shoes were invented and used, and I've always found them to be a tool of protection for the hoof, however, you must be very diligent about keeping to a strict schedule of shoe removal, re-trim, re-fit, and then putting the shoes back on, and sometimes just letting the hoof rest without shoes. The hoof can outgrow the shoe! On the other end, I've seen some horrid cases where the unshod, neglected hoof grew up and over the top of the hoof itself and curved upwards to a point! People who let this happen to their horses should be punished at sunrise! I've seen such bad cracks that metal bars had to be put over them to stop crack continuance. I think I've probably seen a lot more hoof damage than I've cared to see in my lifetime. As I stated previously, I only speak for myself and I've always kept shoes on all of my horses other than one who had wonderful hooves and who wasn't ridden on bad surfaces. There are the wild Mustangs who've run their hooves down on natural terrain for decades and never needed to be shod. This is called "natural conditioning" and works fine with them. However, the hoof is made of keratin, and if a horse is kept in boggy pastures, urine-soaked stalls, and in generally unfit conditions, this keratin, (a layered protein and not bone,) can quickly weaken and become soft and fragile. So... there's a lot more to horse ownership and foot care than most people realize. I can only hope that when you decide to have your own horse, you will apply common sense in your approach to complete horse care. There are many great books available to learn from that give a common sense approach to complete horse care. Being no Shakespeare, "To Shoe Or Not To Shoe" is a question the great writer may have never pondered, but I, the sometime Bard, very much do question. A great website to visit, where you can look through the many wonderful books they have to offer, is: Trafalgarbooks.com, who have a large inventory of high-quality horse books from which to choose. The covers are professional and beautifully done, and they immediately caught my attention. These books will take you down the trail from horse adventures to horse know-how. Your wee ones will fall in love with "Fergus," the cartoon horse who has many tales to tell. Trafalgar Square Books is a woman-owned publishing company located in the drop-dead gorgeous countryside of Vermont.

No matter your choice of whether to shoe your horse or have it go barefoot, please ensure you'll do the best that is indicated for your horse, and who is one of the most wonderful creatures anyone can have the pleasure of "owning," and the privilege of writing about! Keep in mind, yes, we pay for them, pay for their upkeep and health, and pay a lot for them if they are of good bloodline, but we can never really "own" such a magnificent creation as the horse! I'd add further that the hoof can be the most vulnerable part of the horse!

Lady Mo Pascoe-Hoyal

Photo Credit:

Mo Pascoe – Hoyal.

Chapter 28
Queen Elizabeth II And Her
Undying Love Of Horses

It was a bright, sunny day in Hyde Park in Central London at 10:43 a.m., on July 20, 1982, when fifteen beautiful horses from the "Household Cavalry" walked in perfect unison down the south carriage drive. Suddenly, a huge explosion ripped through the morning air. A massive bomb had been placed in a parked car adjacent to the roadway. Another bombing also occurred at Regent's Park, 2.8 miles from Hyde Parkway. "The explosions killed eleven military personnel: four soldiers of the Blues and Royals at Hyde Park and seven bandsmen of the Royal Green Jackets at Regent's Park. Seven of the Blues and Royals' horses were also killed in the attack. One seriously injured horse, Sefton, survived and was featured on television programmes and was awarded 'Horse of the Year.'" (Quotation from Wikipedia)

I distinctly remember this day with great sorrow. Although not confirmed, many say Queen Elizabeth II was the I.R.A.'s intended target. There are a lot of people in Britain who are animal lovers. The sight of these magnificent animals strewn over the roadway was visualized by many who will never forget. These horses were going to the "Changing of the Guard Ceremony."

Horses are an integral part of the royal family. When the late Queen Elizabeth was alive, she had several horses for personal use in ceremonies. These horses were named Swift, Sure, Lightness, and Just Fine. However, at one point, the Queen had over 100 horses! Queen Elizabeth also had a keen interest in racing horses. The Queen was given her first horse at age 4 by her father, King George V. She could ride the much-adored Shetland pony by the age of 6!

The Queen took a personal interest in the "Household Cavalry Mounted Regiment." She personally inspected "The Blacks," the color of the ceremonial horses. It was reported the Queen would spot the slightest injury on a horse. Her motivation wasn't the look of the horse for parades; it was more like her love of horses. The Queen's daughter, Princess Anne, shared her mother's passion for riding. Princess Anne was the first royal member to compete in the Olympic games. As a child, I vividly remember Princess Anne competing in a very hard course, including high jumps and water obstacles. I can see her face as she jumped "Goodwill," one of the Queen's horses. I can also remember my family being glued to the television with bated breath. At one point, the princess was thrown from Goodwill into a water obstacle. All of my family got nearer to the tiny TV Screen to see if she and the horse were okay. With care, Anne regained her position in the saddle. With a good heart, Anne patted Goodwill to show there was no problem with what happened. In a later interview, Anne was generous in her praise of Goodwill, putting her spill down to bad luck.

The love of horses was passed down to Princess Anne's daughter, Zara Tindall. Zara was the first Royal to win a silver medal in the 2012 Olympics. The Great British Royal Family also participated in World War I with three Cavalry regiments: The Royal Horse Guards (The Blues). The Blues participated in many of the now legendary battles of the Great War, including Mons, Ypres, Passchendaele, and Sambre. The Royal Horse Artillery fought throughout WWI, not to forget the VII Royal Horse Artillery.

The Queen also bred Shetland ponies at Balmoral Castle in Scotland. At Hampton Court, the Queen oversaw the breeding of Fell Ponies. The Queen also loved horse racing and owned a stud farm at the Royal Sandringham Estate in Norfolk. It was noted that Queen

Elizabeth could tell the "Going" of a horse racecourse just by the sounds of horse's hooves! The Queen's affinity with racehorses is now that of legend. Her most cherished win was with her horse called Estimate. Estimate won the 2013 Gold Cup at Ascot Racecourse. This race was the first Gold Cup won by a reigning monarch's horse in 207 years! A life-size statue of Estimate was commissioned by the Queen. To this day, the statue stands in the main hall at Sandringham Estate.

The 1982 bombing by the I. R. A. targeting our Queen was an outrage. The troubles as they are now known are behind us, thank the Lord. I felt it was only right to delve into the Queen's love and passion for horses. My family owned an Irish pony for a few years. Her name was Tarka. We were only a working-class family. My sister, who owned the pony, had two jobs just to buy the food for her. As the concrete spreads over the lands, it's nice to be able to look back at our great British history and feel a part of the horse community. "If it's good enough for the Queen, it's good enough for us!"

Lord David. L Banks

Chapter 29
Bucky Doodle

His name was just plain old Buck when I bought him from the O'Quinns (Big Mama and Pa Finney) who worked from sunrise until after sunset milking their herd of cows every day of the week. They took me and my young son, still in diapers, under their loving wings, knowing how very homesick I was. They were my real first Louisiana family beside my in-laws. I had traded the sharks of Hawai'i for Southern alligators, which in actuality, are worse than sharks. 'Gators' can get you from the banks of a lake, while sharks can't get you out of the water. The "culture shock" was unbearable for me until when we moved to a farm as overseers for free rent in a little country town called Lecompte, named after a famous Louisiana racehorse. The O'Quinns were quick to take us in, as was the Hickman family, who owned a little grocery store just across the road from the dairy. Both families loved my son and me as though we were kids of their own. Pa Finney sold me a horse for $100.00, and this alone helped even more since I had left horses behind me on my island of Oahu, where I entered horse shows, took care of a string of Polo ponies, and rode every day of my life.

Buck was half Percheron, half Quarter Horse and talk about a combination of bloodlines! He was tall, of course, very filled out, highly muscular, and about as bomb-proof as any horse I had ever ridden. I felt very safe with this grey-brown gentle giant. His disposition was as grand as he was tall. After a while, I called him Bucky Doodle and would sing the Yankee Doodle song to him while riding, changing the words to his name and making up my own lyrics. He seemed to enjoy this and quickly learned that his name was Bucky

Doodle. We traveled many miles together, and his behavior was perfect even as we went along the busy two lane highways to ride from the farm over to visit the O'Quinns and Hickmans. He never even flinched a muscle when a large semi passed by. A lot of times these families would keep my son so I could have a peaceful hour's solo ride. When I became pregnant with my second baby, my sweet, tiny daughter, Buck, would keep us safe as well when we went for a gentle ride. I think she was rocked to sleep inside me by the easy motion of his slow gait. We walked mainly and only trotted minimally.

I do need to mention the day I called Big Mama on the phone and excitedly told her I had shot a turkey! She came over to see a dead Guinea hen that I knew nothing about, as it just looked like a turkey to me. Of course, I was the joke of the year in those families, but Big Mama took the hen home, cleaned it, and fixed us a most delicious Guinea Gumbo for dinner that night! Yes, there was much laughter at the table that evening, with me keeping a red face all the while from blushing. Sadly, we left Lecompte to live as overseers of a huge 1000-acre farm, also with free rent, to be closer to my husband's place of employment. The Doodle came with us since there was plenty of land for both him and little Smoky, the pony I had gotten my little boy the Christmas I was giving birth to his sister two and a half years later. I was able to do a lot of riding at this huge farm and even taught Bucky to put his front hooves up to the top of the fourth concrete step of the back porch and stand there while a photo was taken of us. He was intelligent as well as gentle and I never had another horse so completely safe as he was ever since. There were eight more who followed, along with two more ponies!

Eventually, as my babies became old enough for horse shows and rodeos, I wanted to enter Western Pleasure events again and sold my Bucky Doodle to a friend of mine who worked at the hospital with me. My husband didn't want to keep him for hunting-he'd have made a fine woods horse from which a hunter could shoot. I made sure he went to a good home. In came the $400.00 (million dollar) horse, Sir George. We took first place in every show we entered, except for one second place. I had many good years with him until a divorce separated us. Horse went to another good home, while my children and I went to Nashville where I shopped my songs in Music Row. So ends the story of Bucky Doodle, but I want to tell the whole world that he was the most wonderful horse to have. I sold him for that same $100.00 I paid for him! When I last saw him, he was very happy at his new place and he was surrounded by a "whole passel of grand younguns" who were absolutely devoted to him!

The Doodle wasn't the finest horse I've ever had; he wasn't flashy or high-stepping. I didn't feel he was show material and we may have gotten laughed at had I tried to enter him in a Western Pleasure event, but he gave more to me than any trophy could bring. This gentle giant carried me and my children safely wherever we would go. He never shied, snorted in fear or became hard to handle. The glory I can give to this real regular, but tall horse, was that he took me from the doldrums of home-sickness hell, into a much happier world. A world where I could be kept busy caring for him, and a world that distracted me from such loneliness and heartache. I also left my very young and precious little sister behind when I departed that island which hurt even more. My Paula was seven years my junior and she was a large part of my heart. In hindsight, I should have taken her on more rides because she adored horses too. A lot of guilt felt here, especially when I have too much thinking time, ya, "shoulda, coulda, woulda."

All in all, though, this big hunk of wonder saved my life in a sense, as he kept me safe, happy, and busy. I was back to doing what I had done before leaving my island and trying to be a good young mother. I tried even harder to be mature in my twenties, which was especially difficult because I was still very attached to my Mama, Daddy, and little

Sis back home. Perhaps I succeeded in some ways, though. My grown children are the best a mother can have; they've given me four loving, beautiful grandchildren, and now one of my granddaughters and one grandson have given me three beautiful great-grand babies. What more can a horsewoman expect out of life?

Lady Mo Pascoe-Hoyal

Chapter 30
Trail's End
Afterword

"The Hoof And I" took ten years to write! Why? My new and best computer, a Dell Desktop was struck by lightning indirectly, twice, repaired once and now left to rest on a shelf. I have tons of photos that must be transferred to CD's and still haven't gotten around to doing that. The second computer, a laptop is where most of my book is contained, along with all of my newer photos. I was able to remove some stories from a third old computer and several stories are now on my new Dell Desktop. From this day forward, all new articles, stories and another book that is nearly half way done, will all be contained in this Dell. I was locked out for many years and couldn't get into two laptops other than to make copies of stories. I couldn't edit until I bought a wireless printer. Oh blessed and beautiful God up in Heaven, my whole world then opened and this printer now enables me to use any computer from here to eternity. Since this miracle in technology occurred, I scurried like "The Mad Hatter" to finish this book, with the deadline of December 31, 2024. I didn't want to go into the year 2025 with it, but it did in spite of what I wanted. I remained so frustrated for many years, not being able to complete this book. One thing I learned about what happened to new Dell computer and our lovely floor style television by the front living room window, also "blasted," was that our front yard contains a lot of iron that attracts lightning. Anything at the front of this house is subject to being struck even though the strike doesn't enter the house, thankfully! Stupid me who thought a power surge strip would be a cure all, it wasn't, and now I unplug anything necessary when I hear the first peal of thunder.

So what's all this gabbing got to do with horses? It had a world to do with them because I couldn't finish this book all about them. Now that I'm finally finished, I sigh with relief that most of my writing world is in much better order, and it's just me who isn't! I can only work a very few hours at a time due to many injuries, the most painful was the fracturing of the coccyx, sitting is brutal for pain and then the burning that sets in after trying to do anything for even one half hour. Is anyone crying yet? I hope not.

Arthritis in the wrong places or any place at all is a life changer. It's insidious and can be very disabling. I do understand that many people suffer with it. I am so, so sorry you have to go through such pain, limitation and loss of mobility. My heart goes out to all who suffer, no matter the cause, and only those who suffer can truly understand the suffering of others. IF I could have this tailbone removed, perhaps most of the pain would go away. My Orthopedic surgeon looked into this matter and told me that no doctor in the state of Louisiana does this kind of surgery. It can be dangerous due to the proximity of the colon and there is also is a high risk for infection.

So...that's the end of it for me since I decided at 80 years of age, NO MORE SURGERIES after 22 too many. You'll see in quite a few of my stories, that I've mentioned disability so many times, I'm truly sorry. I haven't meant to bore you or make this all about myself, although this is my book! However, when anyone loves to work as much as I do, especially craving manual labor, and me who has been used to doing it all of my life, starting before the age of 9, left me with a big hole in my soul because I am no longer able to do it. Shoveling out a stall and a large paddock was pure happiness for me. Grooming, feeding and riding my horses brought a lifetime of pleasure, only to have it all suddenly jerked right out from under me. It was like someone killing me, only I didn't die, other than internally. I had to trade my wonderful Australian saddle seat for this black office chair with an extra pillow that has a V-shape cut out of its back to give pressure relief. Guess what? It doesn't work! I continue to be stubborn as a mule and won't give in to the pain, and I fully intend on writing for the rest of my life. I hope you will enjoy this book, notice the intelligence in writing from all the contributors, while being able to fully comprehend it as there are no put ons, or hoity-toity writers, only those who are gentle souls and much loved by me. I want to take this opportunity to thank all who donated their great stories which nicely increased the volume of this work. I did have a total of nine horses and three ponies in my lifetime but not all of them were subject matter for stories. Without the guest writers listed on the first page, this book would not have been possible, so a big thank you to each and everyone of you! I am very grateful. My eternal gratitude also goes out to my loving sister and Senior Editor, Paula Abbott. Without her this book would be a punctuation and grammatical mess! Add mild dyslexia!

After many battles throughout my life and the many chapters I have lived, I feel there will be scads of other ideas and issues to write about once this book is done. My perpetual Novena to Our Lady of

Lourdes is helping me tremendously with my writing and I know she'll help with this book!

In the meantime, I'll continue to collect just one more story from England and get that edited. My sister and I are still "in the saddles" together, it's just that we ride a different kind of horse these days. Paula is, and has always been, "My Constant" all of my life and I am very grateful to and for her.

Any and all riding has now ended and is very sadly missed. Gone are my mare and pony which is even worse. I am very thankful to Ginger and her husband, Daryl Schouest, who drove the 140 mile round trip to pick them up to adopt my babies, taking them to their ranch. Daryl eased my heartache by telling me, "They are just going on a vacation." He will never realize how much those sweet words of comfort still carry me though the anguish of losing them. Their beautiful Patterson family followed along for our very sad reunion. Daughter Amanda, beautiful like her Mother, grandchildren Ayden and Faith Ann, I love you all so much! Lolly and Ranger will have the best of care and they can gorge on the verdant grass growing at the Camelot Wilderness Ranch, in Leonville, Louisiana. This couple has done the best favor of any favors I've ever received so far, other than my Mother giving me life! Thank you so much my beautiful Gigi and handsome gentleman, Daryl. May your trails never come to an end!

Writing my first book, "The Hoof And I" has been an act of love, and a book I've been needing to write for a long time. I am finally seeing fruition. I am blessed, I am grateful! "Creativity is God-given, and those who ignore such gifts are doomed to unhappiness." Kris Kristofferson. No truer words could ever have been spoken!

"Be happy" were the last two words said to me by my precious Mother as she lay dying. Yes, my beautiful Mama, I will be happy! I think I will leave it at that!

I am proud to inform you that Joshua Harris, Chloe Cooper, Luke Davis, and my Angel, Jennifer Bloom of Book Marketeers have helped me tremendously in the publishing this book. They have become co-workers and sweet friends! The Staff at Book Marketeers are kind, very patient, extremely professional, and I am so grateful for you whom I'll always consider to be my friends. Thank you so very much!

Not The End, Only The Beginning

Photo Credit

Pete Ferington

About the Author

Mo Pascoe-Hoyal was born and raised in Honolulu, Hawaii, daughter to Charles and Eleanor Pascoe. While residing there, Mo was an award-winning Equestrian. She was also a member of The Screen Extras Guild with movies to her credit.

Mo is also a published songwriter in Nashville and New York. She now resides in Central Louisiana where she has retired and is now a published writer.

Mo is the very proud Mother of son, Michael, and daughter, Jodiah. She has four grandchildren: Cameron, McKenzie, Shaylee and Reece. Add three great grandchildren: Emery, Blaze and Aurabella, whom she considers to be her best achievements of all.

In 2014, Mo was made Lady Mo Pascoe-Hoyal of Glencoe, Scotland and is very proud of her title as Lady!

Mo wishes God to Bless each one of you!

Photo Credit: Wayne E. Hoyal

www.ingramcontent.com/pod-product-compliance
Lightning Source LLC
Chambersburg PA
CBHW071800120626
46550CB00002B/861